P R A C T I C A L

SAILING

PRACTICAL SAILING

TIMOTHY JEFFERY

GALLERY BOOKS
An imprint of W.H. Smith Publishers Inc.
112 Madison Avenue
New York, New York 10016

A QUINTET BOOK
produced for
GALLERY BOOKS
An imprint of W.H. Smith Publishers Inc.
112 Madison Avenue
New York, New York 10016

ISBN 0-8317-7072-4

This book was designed and produced by
Quintet Publishing Limited
6 Blundell Street
London N7 9BH

Art Director: Peter Bridgewater
Designer: Linda Moore
Editor: Shaun Barrington
Illustrators: Rob Schone, Trevor Ridley
Lorraine Harrison

Typeset in Great Britain by
Central Southern Typesetters, Eastbourne
Manufactured in Hong Kong by Regent Publishing
Services Limited
Printed in Hong Kong by Leefung-Asco
Printers Limited

Picture credits: a = above, b = below, l = left, r = right

BRITISH SEAGULL COMPANY: 47ar; EYELINE PHOTOS AND FEA-
TURES: 17al, 18 (centre) 19br, 64 (centre), 94, 96; TIMOTHY
JEFFERY: 13, 16ar, 20, 22al, 23, 25, 29, 33, 34, 35, 38, 41, 43ar,
46, 48, 52r, 53al, 54b, 56, 57al/ar, 58al, 60al, 61, 69, 71, 74-
80al, 81br, 82, 83, 84bl, 85, 86, 89l, 91, 97, 104; YACHTING
WORLD: 9-12, 15, 19ar, 22ar/r, 26, 27, 37, 42, 45, 50, 51,
52al, 54a, 55al, 57br, 58bl, 59, 60r, 62-67, 68, 70, 73al/ar/r,
80 (centre), 81ar, 84a, 87, 88, 89r, 90, 92 (centre), 95ar, 99,
100, 101, 107.

EDITOR'S NOTE

Sailing is a sport which is dependent on the
forces of nature. Because of the vagaries of
wind and water and the various challenges
posed by different localities, no single volume
can prepare an individual for all eventualities
when sailing. The producers and author of this
book therefore strongly advise the reader to
enrol in a certified course of instruction, so that
he or she is fully prepared to participate safely.

C O N T E N T S

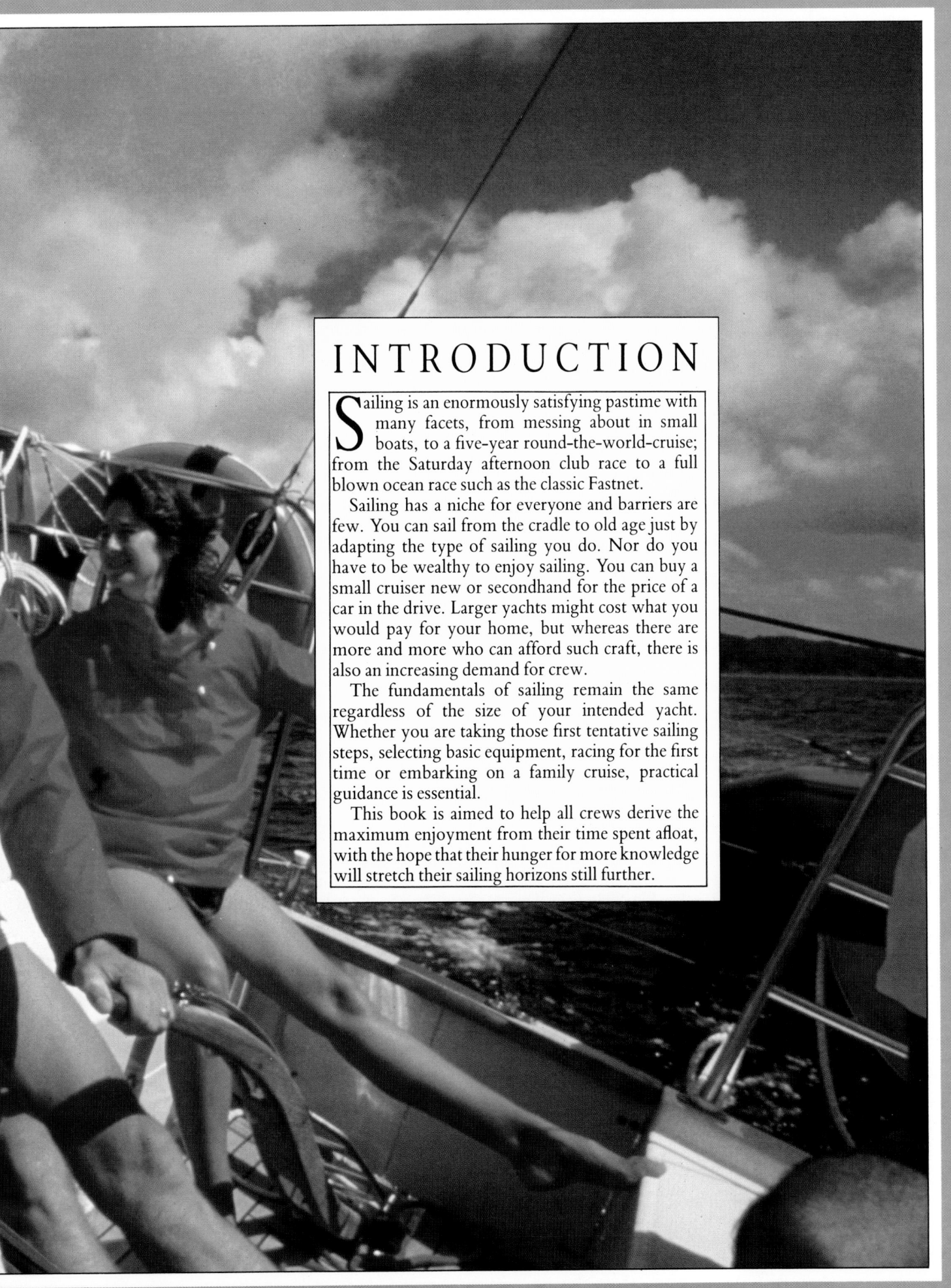

INTRODUCTION

Sailing is an enormously satisfying pastime with many facets, from messing about in small boats, to a five-year round-the-world-cruise; from the Saturday afternoon club race to a full blown ocean race such as the classic Fastnet.

Sailing has a niche for everyone and barriers are few. You can sail from the cradle to old age just by adapting the type of sailing you do. Nor do you have to be wealthy to enjoy sailing. You can buy a small cruiser new or secondhand for the price of a car in the drive. Larger yachts might cost what you would pay for your home, but whereas there are more and more who can afford such craft, there is also an increasing demand for crew.

The fundamentals of sailing remain the same regardless of the size of your intended yacht. Whether you are taking those first tentative sailing steps, selecting basic equipment, racing for the first time or embarking on a family cruise, practical guidance is essential.

This book is aimed to help all crews derive the maximum enjoyment from their time spent afloat, with the hope that their hunger for more knowledge will stretch their sailing horizons still further.

CHAPTER ONE

GOING AFLOAT

A new yacht can be bought direct from the builder at a boat show, from sales offices or an agent. Secondhand yachts are available from brokers who act on behalf of the seller, or from the seller direct, via advertisements on club notice-boards or in sailing magazines.

Whatever means you use, try to get a second opinion. If you are buying a new boat, talk to existing owners. Secondhand yachts are not fully protected by consumer legislation so the answer is to have a survey done. Do not be put off by the cost. In the vast majority of cases the money is well spent.

Knowing what you are looking for and can afford will narrow down the choice, so work out clearly the type of sailing you intend to do, where the yacht will be kept and where you would like to take her.

Wooden yachts are much less common today, and yachts built expressly to customer requirements even less so. Economies of large-scale production mean that today's models come off the lines in standard form. This is not to say that the choice is less than it was 30 years ago; yachting was a smaller sport then. Modern yachts are both fast, under sail and power, and offer many creature comforts below.

THE CRUISER-RACER

This is probably the most common production yacht today. Hull design is often sporty and drawn with an eye on a measurement rule such as the International Offshore Rule (IOR). Such yachts are often not only beamy but carry their beam well aft to allow large 'quarter' berths in a small yacht and after cabins in large ones.

Displacement is moderate and the underbody will have a deep fin keel which makes up for its small lateral area with a high-lift foil section to resist sideways 'slip' or leeway. The rudder will be a deep 'spade' at the after end of the hull – the characteristic 'fin-and-skeg'.

Yachts like these need to be sailed fairly upright to keep their narrow bow/wide stern form in balance, but they have both speed and good interior volume.

CRUISING YACHTS

Cruisers are designed with no racing rule in mind. Generally they will be slower in light air and off the wind in heavy air, but capable of good average speeds. Displacement (weight) will be greater, and this will produce a less jerky motion and an ability to carry the extra weight of fuel, water and stores necessary for long distance cruising.

Some of the extra displacement will be carried in the keel which may well be the old style long keel which runs all the way aft and carries the rudder on its trailing edge. More modern designs have a separate keel and rudder, though the keel is still fairly long and the rudder will usually be mounted on a full length supporting skeg to protect it.

The longer keel will also help to support the yacht when she 'dries out'.

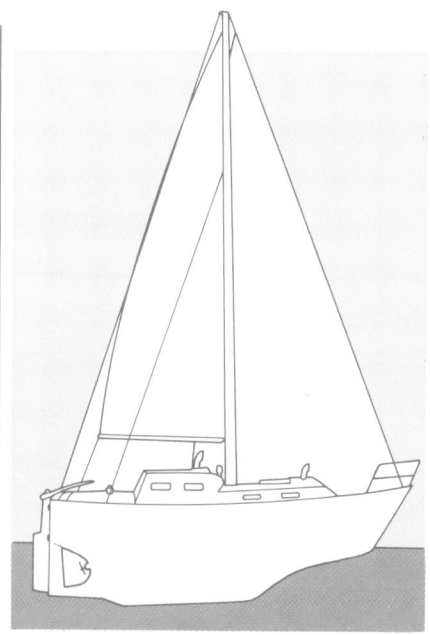

ABOVE *An ocean cruiser with heavy displacement. Note the full keel and large rudder hung on the transom. The rig is masthead sloop.*
OPPOSITE *A cutter rigged foretriangle.*

ABOVE *A modern version of the full keel design, with sleeker lines. The rudder is still hung on the aft edge of the keel. This is a cutter rig, as two jibs are set rather than a single, bigger headsail.*
BELOW RIGHT *A half-ton class yacht, this a pure racer.*

PURE RACING YACHTS

Racing yachts have light displacement and more complex rigs. They can be designed to a rating rule so that they compete with different yachts for corrected results on handicap, or they may be identical yachts for first-across-the-line racing. The latter are known as 'one-designs' where hull shape and weight are strictly controlled. Owners may be allowed some variation in deck gear and sails, or none at all.

Racing yachts designed to the International Offshore Rule are sailed in events such as the famous Admiral's Cup ocean racing series. The J24 is perhaps the best-known one-design in the world.

MULTIHULLS

Yachts with two or three hulls have a small but loyal following. Whereas monohulls rely on ballast in their keels for stability, catamarans and trimarans use their very wide beam.

Multihulls may be sluggish in light air and may not be very close-winded, but they are capable of high speed and fast passage-making. They offer plenty of deck space, good room below and a platform which heels little.

TRAILER-SAILERS

Some small yachts (up to 25ft (8m) for example) are designed to be trailed. This means you do not have to have a permanent mooring afloat and the boat can be brought home at the end of the season.

Trailing such yachts needs a larger than average car and the launching, recovery, rigging and derigging is both time consuming and hard work.

The reality of trailing your yacht to the water is not as easy in practice as the theory might suggest, but the ability to move a small racing boat around from regatta to regatta and the possibility of bringing her home at the end of the season is attractive nonetheless.

KEELS

The 'winged' keeled *Australia II*'s historic win of the America's Cup in 1983 has generated much interest in keel design. More and more boatbuilders are offering different keel options.

The main choices are twin or bilge keels, lifting keels, centreboards or the patented Scheel keel. Twin keels allow yachts to dry out upright. If your mooring dries out between tides or your sailing is in shallow water, keels like these are extremely useful. Some builders fit twin rudders also, to keep the boat level. A lifting keel generally retracts right into the hull. An easy-to-operate mechanism is needed. Such keels intrude into the cabin space and cost more.

Centreboards are usually housed in a stub keel, and in light air are both efficient upwind owing to their foil shape and downwind because they can be retracted to reduce wetted surface.

Perhaps the best compromise for a shoal draught keel, is that designed and patented by American Henry Scheel. Despite its lack of depth, the Scheel is belled out at its bottom to concentrate ballast low down and its subtle shaping also produces efficient lift.

RIGS

The most common rig today is the Bermudan sloop. Such rigs are described as masthead, when the mainsail and headsails are hoisted to the top of the mast, or fractional, when the forestay is connected part way up the mast.

Larger yachts may carry a second mast at the stern, the mizzen and are called ketches if the mizzen is stepped forward of the rudder post or yawls if it is abaft of it.

A yacht with two masts, either of the same height or if the after one is higher, is called a schooner. If there is both an inner and outer forestay to allow two headsails to be carried, then it is known as a cutter.

Free-standing masts (ie with no shrouds or stays) are called 'Freedom' rigs, but they are not very common.

ABOVE *This is the older style ketch rig, with the sail plan split between a large mainsail and a smaller mizzen, mounted aft. The hull has a separate keel and rudder, although there is still lots of volume (displacement) in the underbody.*
BELOW LEFT *Finishing a tack, the crew must re-set the headsail as the wind spills from it.*

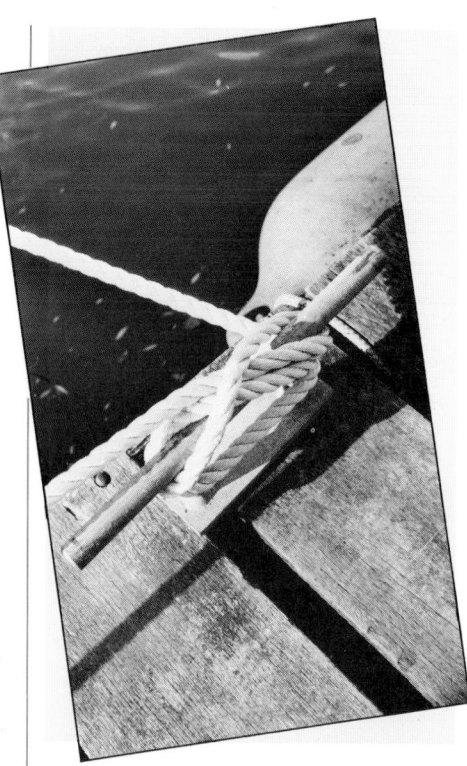

ABOVE *A dock line securely made fast to a mooring cleat with a locking turn.*
OPPOSITE ABOVE *Mooring bow-to. Note the fender amidships suspended from the guard rails. It is better to use an eyebolt fitted specially for the purpose.*
OPPOSITE BELOW *A Dutch marina.*

BERTHS

The problem of where to keep a yacht faces every boatowner but a lot depends on the type of yacht, the availability of moorings and the frequency of use.

The vast increase in the popularity of boating has made finding a place to keep your boat difficult. Rivers which had free, swinging moorings 25 years ago will probably now have well-developed marinas if they are in popular sailing areas or are close to towns or cities. The difference in annual berthing charges is likely to be great although marinas offer convenience and a wider range of services.

MARINA BERTHS

For many people, the marina is the most convenient place in which to keep a yacht. They are generally built in sheltered water such as harbours and rivers and they offer walk-on-board convenience. Sailing gear and provisions can be loaded from the car into a trolley and wheeled right alongside the yacht.

There are many other benefits too, not least of which is some sort of security. This covers everything from having staff to make good a chafed-through warp, to 24-hour vigilance against theft of the yacht and removable gear such as liferafts.

A good marina may also have water, electricity and telephone supplied for each berth; a chandlery and shop; a mobile hoist and crane for lifting yachts and spars; a repair yard; a water and fuel berth; toilet and showers; a launderette; a transportation service linked with the local sail loft, and in the more recent developments, a bar, restaurant, boutique and even apartments and villas.

The berths themselves may be full length or just short finger pontoons to permit a greater density of yachts. In either case, securing the yacht and guarding against chafe is important. Instead of belaying the mooring warps directly to cleats or fairleads, some berth owners attach a short length of chain so that warps clear the pontoon edge. At the other end, attached to the yacht, good fairleads are vital. They should have a soft radiused section free of any edges. If there is any edge at all it will do surprising damage to unprotected rope because a yacht never stays still. Even when made fast, a boat will always be on the move. Some owners make up special fixed dock lines, shackled at one end to the pontoon, covered with anti-chafe PVC tubing where they lie across the yacht and with a loop or bite spliced into the free end ready to slip over the yacht's own cleats.

Fenders are vital to protect the topsides from marking but they should hang at the correct height. It is common practice to suspend them from the guard rails but this puts undue strain on them and it is better to use stanchion bases or specially fitted eyebolts. Owners anxious to preserve their topsides' finish will suspend a soft canvas sheet between the hull and the fenders and add extra fenders to the head and edges of the pontoon. If the yacht is particularly beamy amidships, it could pay to invest in two large spherical fenders to place either side of the widest point with ordinary fenders in between.

Even yachts with relatively straight sides and a narrow beam are awkward shapes to tie up. Obviously bow and stern have to be secured; warps that lead forward and aft from the yacht to the shore are called head (or bow) and stern lines. Those that lead at right angles to the yacht are known as breast ropes but they do little to stop the yacht surging backwards and forwards – so springs have to be used too. One leads aft from a point between the bow and amidships to the shore (bow spring), and another forward from between the stern and amidships to the shore (stern spring).

In general the springs should be taut with the breast, bow and stern lines a little slack. If the berth is in a tidal river and the springs are attached as above, (instead of both sharing one cleat amidships), it should be possible to adjust the lines so that the water flow lifts the yachts slightly away from the pontoon – a much better arrangement than being pinned hard onto it.

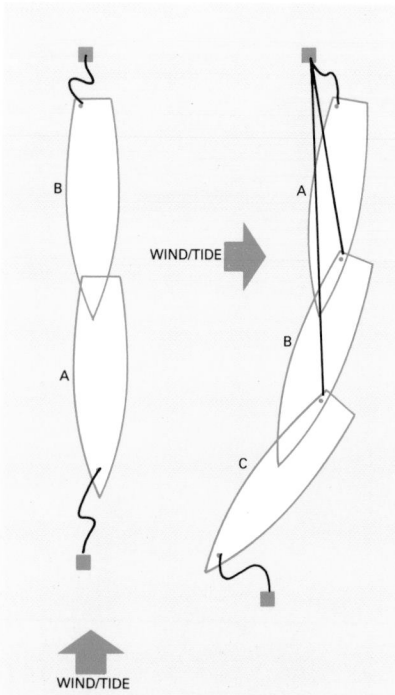

SWINGING MOORINGS

To many sailors, the yacht nodding gently at her mooring buoy in an idyllic setting epitomizes the attraction and freedom of boat ownership. However, swinging moorings have their own problems. They are often laid in an open roadstead subject to high winds and rough seas, or in a small harbour with fishing boat or ferry traffic, or in an area with only enough water to float keel boats at high water.

In the latter case a bilge keel or lifting keel arrangement is necessary, although fin keelers with drying-out legs rigged either side may also take the ground. All yachts need a decent bow roller. The requirements here are high cheeks, a secure 'keep' pin and fittings of stout enough construction and attachment to take the load of a yacht surging up and down in rough weather or lying across the wind or tide.

Backing this up should be a samson post. The advantage of such a fitting, as opposed to a cleat, is that chain can be made fast to it in such a way that it can be released under load. Take two turns around the post or bollard and then pass a loop underneath the taut chain and slip it over the post.

The problem of making chain fast can be simplified by having a ready-made loop in the end which can be passed over a cleat or post. Usually the mooring pick-up buoy will have a short length of rope between the buoy and the chain and this can be made up over the loop to make it doubly secure.

The pick-up buoy should be marked with the yacht's name and, if you are

ABOVE *Pile moorings. Attach the bow line first (left), then drop to secure the stern before adjusting lines to bring the yacht to mid-point between the piles. With wind and/or tide abeam (right), attach the stern line first. Then motor forward into the wind or tide to attach the bow line before centralizing the yacht.*
RIGHT *A pontoon moorings, showing fenders and dock lines.*

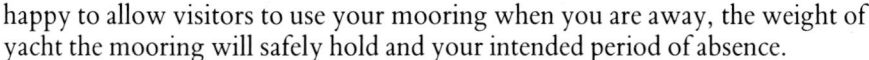

ABOVE LEFT *Swinging moorings.*
ABOVE *A modern 28-footer (8.5 m), with a fractional sloop rig.*

happy to allow visitors to use your mooring when you are away, the weight of yacht the mooring will safely hold and your intended period of absence.

A useful addition is a second smaller buoy attached to the main mooring buoy, weighted at the bottom and with a light pole protruding from the top which can be grabbed so that the mooring buoy can be brought alongside. Other tricks of the trade include using a patented boat hook which latches a line onto the buoy automatically and the padding of the chain with PVC tubing to prevent it damaging the yacht's topsides when it rides over the mooring buoy at the turn of the tide.

All manner of objects have been used as weights on the sea bed – old engine blocks, concrete-filled tyres and old mill wheels. The important thing is that the weight, or anchor mooring, should be heavy enough for the yacht and for local conditions. The chain attached to it should be of the correct diameter too. Just like the yacht herself, the mooring will require regular inspection and maintenance. The chain should be galvanized and tested. Any shackles in the system should be wired up to prevent accidental loosening.

Moorings are usually under the control of a yacht or harbour authority who control their laying and density.

PILE MOORINGS

These are an intermediate step between marinas and swinging moorings. They permit far more boats to be moored in a given area than on the swinging variety but they do not give a marina's walk-on convenience. Piles with metal bars attached to them are driven into the sea or river bed. Running up and down these bars are rings to which the mooring lines are attached. As a yacht rises and falls with the tide, so the warps slide the rings up and down. Often two yachts lie between each set of piles and if they moor bow to stern their masts should be well clear of each other in case wash from a passing vessel causes them to rock together. However, other factors may override this, such as the preferred uptide approach to picking up the mooring or consideration of the wind strength.

When lying alongside the yachts sharing the mooring, springs will have to be rigged although each yacht will have her own bow and stern lines.

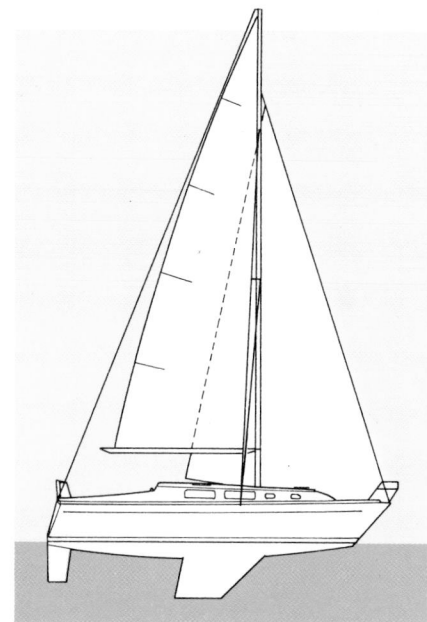

ABOVE *A modern production yacht with medium to light displacement. The hull is sleek with a low wetted surface area. The keel and rudder are efficient foils. The rig is 'fractional', so called because the headsail is hoisted only to a fraction of the height of the mainsail.*
ABOVE RIGHT *Inflatable and rigid type tenders.*

TENDERS

Few yachts can do without a tender. Even if you have a marina berth or a mooring served by a club's launch service, there will always be the need to ferry the crew and stores to and from the shore.

The tender is also useful for working the yacht, laying out a kedge anchor or taking lines away from the yacht to another point. Children will find one an enjoyable diversion, rowing or sailing around an anchorage.

Few dinghies can serve all needs efficiently and most are a compromise.

TYPES OF TENDER

The main distinction here is between rigid and inflatable tenders.

Rigid tenders have been with us for many years and a neat, wooden clinker dinghy hanging in davits is an ideal adjunct to proper cruising. Unfortunately, such dinghies are now very expensive, heavy and can only stow on larger yachts. The modern cruiser has such a large coachroof to give good headroom below that clear deck space is at a premium. If they cannot be carried on deck, then such dinghies must be towed.

If your yacht lies at an exposed mooring a dinghy like this may be the best way to get out from the shore, especially if it is a good rowing dinghy. Rigid tenders are now made in glassfibre and plywood, as well as by traditional construction methods, which helps to reduce their cost.

They will need good fendering to protect your topsides, and metal rub rails underneath to prevent damage when beaching. If you find the dinghy knocking against the yacht, on the turn of the tide for instance, stream a bucket on a warp from the stern of the tender to help hold it clear.

Inflatable dinghies have the great advantage of being easy to stow. Deflated in their valise, they should fit most cockpit lockers, while half deflated they can be rolled up and stowed on deck. They are also very good load carriers and can be brought alongside without fear of damaging the topsides.

They have disadvantages too: firstly, despite being amazingly tough they can be punctured by jagged rocks or sharp projections. Secondly, their mobility and manoeuvrability are poor compared to those of a nicely-shaped rigid tender. They have little directional stability and inertia and they are subject to windage so that they crab around on the surface. In a sea, their high buoyancy makes

ABOVE *The novel 'freedom' rig does not need supporting by shrouds. It is described as free-standing. The sails are worked 'windsurfer-style' with a wishbone boom which fits on either side of each sail.*
ABOVE LEFT *A rigid tender with captive rowlocks, fenders, a pump, and sculling notch.*

them bob up and down, dissipating forward motion, necessitating the curious technique of using short, fast, light rowing strokes rather than the nice, long sweeps characteristic of rigid dinghy rowing.

Yet for all this, inflatables are the answer to many people's needs. Fixed wooden transoms give more shape to the floor and enhance rowing capability as well as making the use of a small outboard motor simple. Floorboards also enhance performance. There is a new generation of folding-floored inflatable which rows, sails and powers surprisingly well, and can even be used as a liferaft when CO_2 inflation and canopy options are specified.

PROPULSION

The art of rowing is well worth mastering and a good rowing dinghy is a joy to use in a scenic anchorage. Longer oars give more propulsion but their length will be governed by the beam of the dinghy (you cannot row cross-handed), and its length (so that they may be stowed inside). If a rigid dinghy is long enough and you have a long row ahead, two thwarts and two rowing positions allow the work to be shared with one crew member handling an oar per side. Heavily loaded inflatables are usually better paddled than rowed.

Be sure that the rowlocks are kept captive in the dinghy so that they are not lost overboard or 'borrowed' in the dinghy park. That said, you would do well to learn the art of sculling. By either holding the oar on the transom, or by using a stern mounted rowlock or notch, you can propel a dinghy forward by sweeping the oar through a figure-of-eight pattern. So efficient is sculling that many French skippers propel their cruising yachts in this way.

If an outboard engine is used, make sure there is a proper transom bracket for it. It should have a lanyard for lashing it to an eyebolt and for added security when it is passed from yacht to dinghy.

Too much power brings no benefit whatsoever. It merely uses more fuel and a large outboard perched on the end of a small dinghy can cause instability. There are some very eager, small, lightweight engines available today producing up to 3.5hp from one cylinder, and offering easy starting. Full gear shift is not necessary for a tender engine.

Because such engines work so close to the water, they should be carefully serviced according to manufacturers' instructions; treat them regularly with WD40, or an equivalent, and if they are stowed on a bracket on the yacht's stern rail, be sure to protect them with a neat canvas cover.

USING A TENDER

Too many mishaps occur on, what is for many, the shortest part of the cruise – the journey from shore out to the yacht. Tenders are unstable due to their size, yet very often they are overloaded with crew not wearing personal buoyancy.

When the tender is launched from either the jetty or the yacht, its painter or tow rope should be made fast, perhaps around a cleat, and led back to whoever is in the dinghy. Normally it is the oarsman who boards first, stepping smoothly into the middle of the dinghy. Other crew members go fore and aft so the tender is loaded evenly. Disembarking is a reverse of this process.

To get underway the outboard oar can be shipped, and when the crew push the tender clear, the inboard can also be shipped. Underway, consideration must be given to wind and tide. Rarely can you aim directly for your destination but rather some distance upwind or uptide from it. You will often see a rower stopping at the transom of the yacht, only to have the tide carry the tender away from the yacht before the crew has made contact.

When approaching the yacht or quay you should aim more or less at the 'target'. With a boatlength to go, unship the inboard oar so that the blade and rowlocks cannot damage the topsides of the yacht. Then with the remaining oar hold the blade in the water so that the tender pivots on it and turns around parallel to the yacht or quay. Get it right, and you will be able to reach out and make the painter fast to finish a neat display of boat handling. More to the point, it prevents ramming the 'target' with the dinghy's bow and stops the crew having to reach ahead from the least stable part of the dinghy.

When towing a tender, make sure every loose item is removed or securely lashed down – oars, rowlocks, bailer, etc. A strong warp should be used for the tow line and secured firmly. Modern, shiny, synthetic ropes can slip on a smooth cleat, especially with the intermittent tugging exerted by the tender. The dinghy attachment must also be strong, a through-bolt on a rigid tender and a strop on an inflatable one.

How long a warp is a matter of experiment. In strong winds an inflatable might have to have a short warp so that the bow is almost brought aboard the yacht, otherwise it will spin crazily in the wind. A rigid tender will surf in a following sea and try and overtake the parent yacht. A long line or a small drogue towed behind the dinghy will help to stop it slewing around.

When you manoeuvre under power, shorten the tow rope right up, or bring the tender alongside to prevent it fouling the propeller.

RIGHT *A Tinker Tramp sailing inflatable.*
FAR RIGHT TOP *Towing the tender behind the yacht in Australia.*

FAR RIGHT BOTTOM *Tenders of course can be fun in safe conditions. A regatta tenders race (ladies class).*

EQUIPMENT

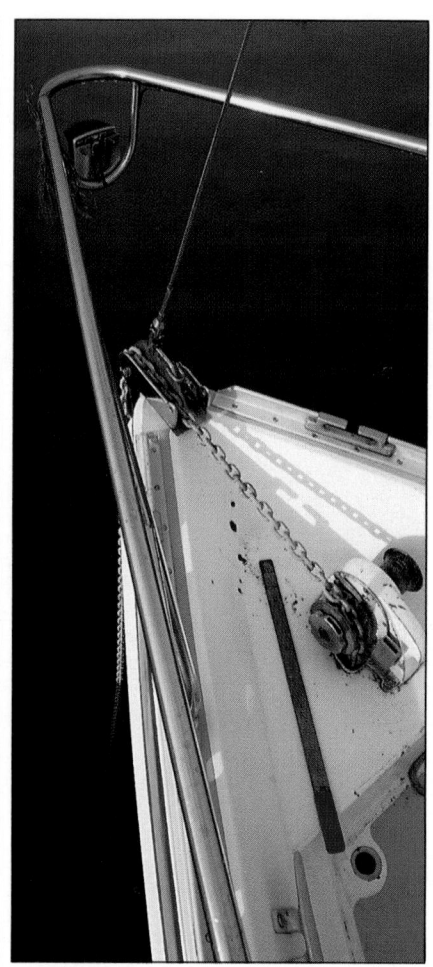

ABOVE *The windlass and chain.*
OPPOSITE *Ensign, horseshoe lifebuoys, and man overboard lights.*

Few yachts today are supplied fully equipped for sea, even if the builders sell them as 'sailaway'. Moreover, secondhand yachts may be better equipped but they will still have gear which is in need of upgrading. The following things ought to be aboard.

BOW ROLLER these need to be stout, yet soft-mouthed and capable of taking sideways load as well as a fore and aft load. A pawl or ratchet can help to raise the anchor chain, by preventing what you have gained slipping back again.

WINDLASS if you anchor with chain, this will be a boon. There should be a reasonably long drop under the hawse pipe to prevent chain jams.

ANCHORS a main bow anchor and alternative style (possibly smaller) kedge are needed. Make sure they are securely stowed. If on the roller or deck chocks, use through-bolts or lashings. If in a bow well, the door should have a clasp.

DECK GEAR large cleats make mooring much easier. If chain is used, they need to be higher off the deck. Cleats amidships will be needed for spring warps and where there is a cleat, a soft-mouthed fairlead is also necessary.

PULPIT a good pulpit will allow a crewman to sit on the lower rail and change sails with his back to the waves. The stern will need similar security from a taffrail or aft pulpit.

GUARDRAILS double guardrails are better than single, and they should be carried on high stanchions secured in firm bases. Guardrails will need secured shackles or bottlescrews at the end in case of accidental collapse, and insulation to avoid 'close loop' radio interference.

WARPS four good length warps will be needed. As a guide, two of them should be one-and-a-half or two times the length of the yacht.

STERN LADDER a transom ladder is useful for boarding high-sided yachts from a dinghy or after a swim. They can also assist with a man overboard. To be of real benefit, the bottom rung should be well below the water's surface when lowered.

MAN-OVERBOARD EQUIPMENT the minimum should be a high-quality horse-shoe buoy, preferably fitted with high-intensity light, whistle and dye marker. A second buoy, a 50-ft (15-m) floating heaving line and a dan-buoy can be added to the list.

HARNESS EYES remaining on deck is vital. There should be safety harness attachment points by the companionway and in the cockpit. Those on the centreline will help stop crew being washed overboard. Jackstays allow a person to move forward from bow to stern. The Latchway Transfastener system is more refined, allowing greater freedom of movement.

NON-SLIP DECKS secure footing is vital to safety, be it on stylish teak, non-slip paint or a proprietary finish such as Treadmaster. Moulded patterns in glassfibre decks are rarely good enough. Watch out for untreated areas on cockpit coamings, cabin tops etc. Forehatches benefit from non-slip tape too.

HANDHOLDS these are vital for secure movement above and below decks. On deck they lead from cockpit to mast, at least; below, they should allow you to operate as normal with 20° of heel.

ABOVE *Fairlead and cleat.*
ABOVE RIGHT *The hull of this yacht is filled with foam to make her unsinkable. Note the navigation lights and lifelines.*
RIGHT *Liferaft and horseshoe buoys are here stored on the transom. Better rafts have double bottoms, large ballast pockets and anti-tangle drogues.*

SAILS the standard mainsail should reef to at least 60% of its normal luff length. Storm sails should also be considered. If the jib is set in a luff foil some alternative means of attachment is a wise precaution.

NAVIGATION LIGHTS showing the correct lights is a legal requirement at night and in poor visibility. Yachts up to 65ft (20m) can use either an electrically efficient masthead tri-light or a bow mounted bi-light combined with a stern light. When motoring, a steaming light is mandatory if the yacht is more than 22ft (7m) in length. This should be carried on the mast and show from full ahead to 22½° aft of the beam. Steaming lights should not be used in conjunction with tri-lights however.

NAVIGATION a VHF radio is both vital for listening to forecasts and a valuable means of summoning help in distress. Both the set and operator must pass official approval. The aerial should be mounted as high as possible for maximum range. A spare emergency aerial is useful in case of dismasting. A cockpit speaker will allow the watch keeper to monitor the radio without disturbing those below. (See equipping the chart table page 36.)

SECURITY BELOWDECKS all heavy items should be secured below against the possibility of a 180° knockdown. This includes cookers. Batteries should be in leak-proof boxes sited out of the engine compartment.

GAS STOWAGE LPG gas is a convenient though potentially volatile fuel. Gas bottles should be stowed in overboard draining lockers. Cookers need flame-failure devices on each burner and all piping should be copper apart from short flexible spans. A shut-off cock at the galley is also needed.

FIRE FIGHTING fire afloat is extremely dangerous and very frightening. All equipment must be sited so that fire in the galley or engine compartment (the most likely fire sources) can be tackled quickly. A fire blanket can smother flame or protect the person. At least three 3lb (1.4kg) extinguishers should be carried. Dry powder types are non-toxic and can be used on all types of fire.

BILGE PUMPS these should be capable of use from the cockpit. Electric pumps should have a manual back-up. A wandering pump will help reach awkward parts, while pick-up pipes need a strainer or strum box to prevent clogging.

FLARES these must be 'in-date' and carried in a waterproof container. Four white and four red hand flares are the minimum for inshore sailing. Offshore, four red parachute flares and two orange smoke flares should be carried as well.

FIRST AID KIT AND MANUAL all items used must be replaced. You will need to deal with seasickness, headaches, upset stomachs, sunburn, constipation and perhaps breakages and flesh wounds.

TOOL KIT pliers, adjustable wrench, spanners, Allen keys, Philips and cross-head screwdrivers, hacksaw, drill and bits will form a good basis. Carry plenty of spares for electrical equipment, the engine, winches and the yacht (blocks, bottlescrews, shackles, self-tapping screws, nuts, bolts, washers etc). Every kit should have PVC or duct tape, WD40 spray or equivalent, sealant and underwater epoxy.

SAIL REPAIR KIT sewing palm, needles, whipping twine, spinnaker repair tape and self-adhesive sail cloth are needed here.

BASIC SAFETY EQUIPMENT

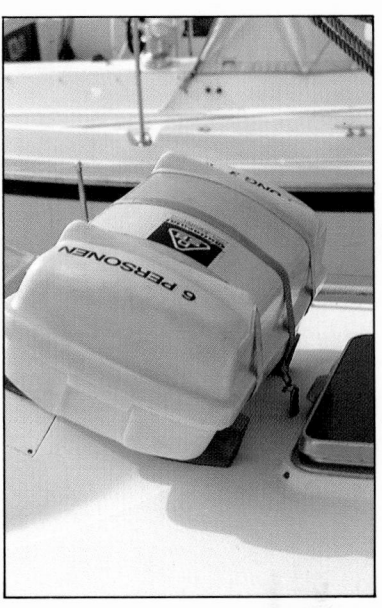

LIFERAFT **A very expensive and probably never-used item. Canister types can stay on deck but valises should be stored in a locker or below, provided that they can be launched in 15 seconds, which is not easy. Alternatives are hiring (if you go offshore just occasionally) or special CO_2 inflatable dinghies.**

SAFETY GEAR **The list is long but includes a fog horn, a radar reflector (above) of at least 90ft² (10m²) echo area, waterproof flashlights, stout buckets with lanyards, bolt croppers in case the mast is lost, and soft wood plugs for driving into fractured hoses and damaged skin fittings.**

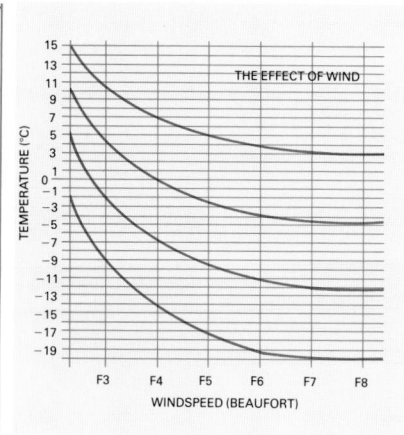

PERSONAL GEAR

Modern sailing clothing bears little or no resemblance to the old heavy yellow oilskins which were often hard to move about in and had dubious water-resistant properties. Layer upon layer was often needed underneath, not so much to keep the warmth in but to add more barriers against the ingress of water.

Today, modern materials have given us stylish, well-designed and highly efficient clothes for sailing. You might be alarmed at the cost but the prices are very competitive when compared with other sporting gear which uses far less sophisticated materials and constructions. The importance of good clothing should not be underestimated. Heat loss is quite marked even in low wind speeds so a wind-proof outer layer is essential. A waterproof layer is vital too, for wet clothing has only 10% of the insulation value of dry clothing.

MATERIALS

The most important insulator is free and available in limitless quantities. It is air, and how it is trapped accounts for much of the thermal property of most materials.

The choice these days is between man-made fibres and natural materials. It is an argument not fully resolved and most sailors find themselves wearing some combination of the two. Eiderdown may offer the greatest heat insulation, up to 90% of its theoretical maximum, but it is very expensive and of little use when it is wet. Wool has long been a favourite, particularly in its oiled form, but it is slow drying and smelly when wet.

Natural materials are still a good foundation until conditions warrant oilskins. Denim jeans are best avoided because once damp they take a very long time to dry. Their close-fitting styling makes kneeling and bending difficult. Lose-fitting trousers, a good thick cotton or wool shirt and pullover are best.

FOUL WEATHER – OILSKINS

Oilskins will most likely be the most expensive purchase and the more you pay the better the garments will be. Oilskin trousers should be chest-high to keep the wind away from the gap between waist-high trousers and the jacket. They should also have a means of securing the ankles to keep out water. A pocket and an opening fly are always useful provided that they do not compromise the trousers' watertight integrity.

Jackets are more convenient if they are zipped at the front rather than being an over-the-head style anorak (windbreaker). There should be flaps both on the inside and outside to seal off the zip. Like the trousers, the wrist opening should be capable of being sealed against the arm. Plenty of pockets are useful for hand-kerchiefs, knives, torches and so on.

As you spend more the garments should offer more refinements: a built-in, close-fitting hood with fasteners rather than ties which are awkward to use with cold hands; a lining to cut down condensation, perhaps even a closed-cell buoyancy lining; hand warmer pockets; a built-in safety harness; crotch strap; reflective patches for man-overboard situations. Top-of-the-range garments will also have reinforced knees, seats and elbows. The manufacturers will have taken special care to cut the garment to avoid seams in highly stressed areas such as the shoulders and seat to ensure they remain watertight.

Oilskins are made in two main types of material: polyurethane-proofed woven nylon and PVC. Woven nylon generally stows more compactly and is more supple and lighter to wear. It needs frequent washing to remove ingrained salt. Some makers offer a winter re-proofing service. PVC is thought to be tougher and more abrasion resistant. Small tears can be taped or welded with glue. Most PVC suits are heavy to wear and carry.

LEFT *The safety harness should be worn on deck in difficult conditions.*
BELOW LEFT *Safety harness tether lines. Note that the bottom hook has a double action to prevent accidental opening.*

ABOVE *The latchway safety system. The transfastener is attached to one of the specially designed fittings.*

FOUL WEATHER – WARM WEAR

For the layer next to the skin, thermal underwear is available. Instead of using cotton, which absorbs body moisture, most manufacturers use something artificial such as polypropylene or actylmer which transfers moisture away – a process known as 'wicking'. When working on deck in oilskins it is very easy to work up a sweat and a moisture-transfer process is a comfortable alternative to cotton. Both T-shirt tops and long-john trousers are available in these materials.

The layer between this foundation and the outer oilskins is often a fibre-pile garment available worldwide – Javlin, Helly Hansen, Land's End, Dorlon and Chuck Roast are just some of the makers. The pile in these garments traps air making them great insulators and now that they often have a finely-woven outer shell, they afford good wind resistance when conditions do not warrant an oilskin jacket.

In warm air and a dry breeze they can dry out in a few hours and even putting them on wet is not unbearable. For overnight sailing, salopette-style trousers can keep the bottom half nice and snug.

If another layer is needed on top, consider a waistcoat. These are now very stylish for après sail and they retain body warmth underneath oilskins without further limiting arm movement.

HEAD, HANDS AND FEET

It is often the extremities which suffer the cold first and for longest. The head can lose as much heat as the body can produce, so something worn up top can make the whole body feel warmer. A skiing-style hat is ideal, while a balaclava is excellent for more extreme conditions.

Hands must be kept warm and protected. Until they are hardened with regular sailing, leather gloves will protect soft palms. Those with open backs do not offer much warmth and, unless there is double thickness on the inside of the palms and fingers, such gloves will have a very short life handling halyards, sheets and anchor cable.

Fingerless gloves will still allow you to tie knots and undo shackles. For longer periods of inactivity a pair of mitts can make even the chilliest of watches a little more comfortable.

As for the feet, there is no substitute for a good pair of boots. They should be high so that you can work on deck or step ashore from a dinghy without filling them up. The soles should afford a good grip and be non-marking. This generally means that flat soles are best so that ankles are not turned as you tread on the irregularities of the deck and its gear.

Many people believe in having boots a size larger than normal footwear. The air space creates insulation and permits the wearing of a thicker or second pair of socks.

As for shoes, most leisure shoes will suffice. The more support they offer, the better. Other points to look for are a good grip and a sole which neither picks up too much debris which is then walked onboard nor marks. Certain running shoes have black soles and are not suitable.

Leather moccasin styles (Docksiders, Topsiders are two of the better known brands) are very popular among sailors and have the advantage that the leather, stitching and other parts are all salt-water resistant.

SAFETY

This basically concerns personal buoyancy and the safety harness. If you are crewing for someone, always take your own so that you can be sure both items are available and in a serviceable condition. The skipper should ensure that safety gear is provided for his crew but there is no substitute for having your own correctly fitting equipment which you know how to operate.

For personal buoyancy, choose either a lifejacket or a buoyancy aid. The difference is explained by their respective names. A buoyancy aid is just a means to keep you afloat though often they are more practical, stylish and still enjoy approval by regulatory bodies.

A lifejacket on the other hand has a sufficient amount of buoyancy correctly distributed behind the head and on the chest to float the wearer face up away from the direction of the oncoming waves even if he or she is unconscious. Lifejackets are bulky so some yachtsmen use gas or oral inflation types which lie flat against the body although they do require a conscious operator if they are to be of any use. Some inflate automatically on contact with water.

Wearing a safety harness should preempt such problems as it aims to keep the wearer attached to the yacht should he stumble or be swept overboard. The harness should be adjusted to fit over oilskins and be easy to don – even in the dark. Choose a make which offers a positive latch on the snapshackle at the end of the lifeline. Gibb make a snapshackle used worldwide, and a catch on it has to be released before the shackle will open, whereas normal snapshackles can open themselves if attached to an eyebolt.

Wearing a harness should be routine at night or in rough conditions. But a cumbersome harness and lifejacket together can interfere in the operation of each other. This is why top-of-the-range oilskins either have built-in flotation as a substitute for a lifejacket or they offer a specially matched lifejacket which attaches to the outside of the jacket. Combine this with a built-in harness and there is no reason not to use personal safety gear as soon as it is needed. Too often, during a sail change for instance, yachtsmen find excuses not to don a harness.

FAIR WEATHER

Preparations are needed for sailing in hot sunny climes too.

Loose-fitting, long-sleeved light shirts are good while long shorts help protect the legs. The sea reflects a great deal of sun, intensifying its burning power. You will find that noses, shoulders, and tops of thighs are particularly vulnerable.

Protection is needed for the skin (sun block) and eyes. A sun visor is restful when looking aloft at the sails and good sunglasses can prevent eye damage from prolonged exposure to the sun.

OTHER GEAR

There are many other useful items to take afloat. Lip salve is good in fair or foul weather. A knife can not only be useful if it is fitted with a shackle key but an essential item of safety equipment in case a rope has to be freed instantly. A personal waterproof torch and a man-overboard light and whistle are essential in case you ever become separated from the yacht. Fortunately such occurrences are very rare but that is no reason for not taking every possible precaution.

ABOVE *Grab rails make the going easier for the crew.*

WEATHER AND NAVIGATION

The seaman knows the language of meteorology, how the elements affect the weather and the limits of his own ability and those of his yacht in dealing with those elements.

CLOUDS

Clouds are excellent indicators of the weather. Generally speaking, it is not looming black clouds which indicate change but wispy and fibrous white/grey clouds. They are often a portent of deteriorating conditions and the faster they move the sooner the change can be expected.

CUMULUS CLOUDS separate, flat-based and with little vertical height, they usually denote fair weather.

STRATOCUMULUS these are dense and form large banks giving rise to complete cloud cover.

STRATOS a low mist-like cloud which in fair conditions can produce a sea fog.

NIMBOSTRATOS rain-bearing clouds associated with fronts and giving steady rain.

CUMULONIMBUS deep shower and thunder clouds. They mark unstable conditions and often have the characteristic anvil head.

PRESSURE

Areas of low pressure are known as cyclones or depressions. They occur when air rises from low levels to high levels and is cooled. This causes both clouds and precipitation. High pressure areas, or anticyclones, have descending air which warms as it falls, dispersing cloud and inhibiting precipitation.

Weather maps are very similar to land relief maps where, instead of the contours joining points of the same height, they run between points with the same barometric pressure.

'Lows' are shown on the weather chart as areas of low pressure surrounded by isobars with ascending air. A 'high' often has its rings of isobars spaced much further apart.

Due to the earth's rotation the wind blows anticlockwise around a low and clockwise around a high in the northern hemisphere. The wind's path closely corresponds to the isobars and the closer their spacing the stronger the wind. In the southern hemisphere the directions are reversed, and close isobars of course still indicate strong wind.

LOW PRESSURE SYSTEMS depressions are born when two different air masses meet. Then, air pressure drops as a cyclonic circulation occurs like a spiral winding itself up. A 'low' in the northern hemisphere will advance eastwards drawing in warm, subtropical air as it goes. The boundary of the warm air is marked by the warm front, while the cold air behind the cold front tries to overtake it. When the cold air finally overtakes the warm air and curls around it, the front is said to be occluded. Such fronts are characteristic of old and dying depressions.

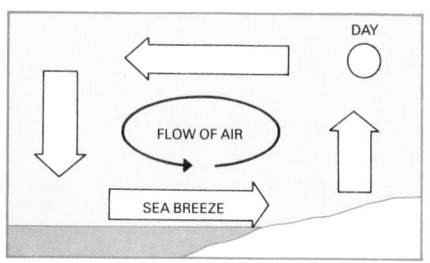

ABOVE *The flow of air which creates a sea breeze. As air rises from the land warmed by the sun, cooler air is drawn in off the sea. This in turn is warmed, rises, cools as it gains height and falls again over the sea.* OPPOSITE *Consulting the chart in perfect weather.*

HIGH PRESSURE SYSTEMS for continental Europe and certain coasts of North America and Australasia, high pressure can bring settled spells of weather. A slack pressure gradient allows winds to be created by other factors with temperature the most frequent cause. Sea breezes often blow in coastal areas, especially during spring and summer. Sea breezes are a consequence of the sun warming the land more than the water causing the air above the land to expand and rise. The air above the sea is sucked in to fill the void.

A slack pressure gradient and convection aided by cumulus cloud helps the creation of sea breezes. Often these blow in mid to late afternoon, lasting until mid evening. The sea breeze may have to overcome an existing wind and there may be a pronounced wind shift, as much as 180°, as the new breeze establishes itself.

In temperate latitudes, sea breezes usually blow at 10–15 knots although they may be stronger given a hot hinterland such as those found in Western Australia and around the Gulf of Mexico.

It is common for coasts to experience sea breezes by day and for a wind to blow from the land by night. This effect is most pronounced in temperate latitudes in spring and summer but sea breezes dominate tropical, and other regions, all year round.

Land breezes are caused by the reverse effect of a sea breeze. Because of this diurnal pattern yachts on passage may find it easier to leave port and clear the coast in the early morning and arrive, with a good tail wind, in mid to late afternoon.

Another type of wind is the katabatic variety, which sinks under gravity and boosts the land breeze. Together with its opposite, anabatics which are upslope winds, these breezes produce puzzling and highly localized conditions. Anabatics blow onto slopes on sunny mornings, drawing air away from those slopes left in shadow. On their way up the slopes, they precipitate moisture. Once at the top, the cold, dense air spills over the peak and sinks down the other slope by gravity rather like a katabatic wind. This wind warms as it tumbles down due to increasing pressure and it rushes out over plains and the sea.

The point for sailors to note is that only a slight pressure gradient is needed for such winds as they gain their strength from temperature change caused by strong sun in hilly terrain. The Mistral, for instance, can exceed gale force, so it is a wind to be cautious of.

THUNDERSTORMS

The earth, rather like a domestic electricity system, has its own flow of electricity – between the surface and the atmosphere. Thunderstorms are discharges to equalize that flow.

In tropical areas, thunderstorms occur with great frequency while in temperate latitudes they may be caused by an unstable airmass or be the precursor to a front. Whatever the cause, thunderstorms are marked by the sudden upward rush of warm, moist air reaching great heights. Unstable air masses will be charged unevenly electrically and equalization is needed. Lightning is the discharge which reestablishes an electrical equilibrium. An observer at sea can easily judge how far away a storm is. Sound at sea level travels at 720 mph (1150 kph), so a five-second gap between a lightning flash and a thunderclap means that the storm is a mile (1.6 km) away.

There is a marked effect on the wind in such storms because the unstable airmass feeds on air drawn in at the bottom which is later dissipated in the storm itself. If the storm formation is to windward of your position, the air being sucked into the base will cancel out the prevailing wind so producing the lull before the storm. As it builds, winds will rush in from the direction of the storm. With the storm downwind of your position the suction effect increases

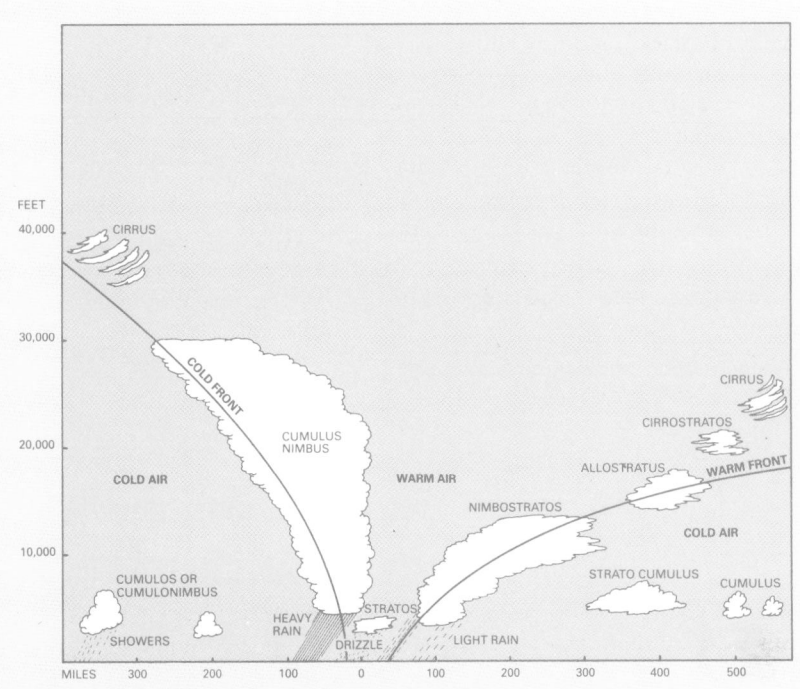

ABOVE *A vertical section through a depression.*

the prevailing wind prior to the calm and then the storm itself. Such storms are usually a summer phenomenon and rarely last more than an hour. They should hold little threat for a yacht because they give ample warning of the possible need to reduce sail and cope with reduced visibility.

The photograph (LEFT) shows a squall building. Lightning strikes are rare and if your yacht has its rig earthed to the keel bolts and skin fittings such a strike should do no damage other than fusing the electrical instruments.

One type of thunderstorm however may be more severe than others. This is the single cell storm which can grow against a strong prevailing wind. If thunder is heard in near gale force winds, a cold front may well be the cause: a sharp wind veer (in the northern hemisphere) will probably occur with squally conditions and confused sea.

FOG

Reduced visibility is of great concern to the small craft navigator. Fog and mist are one and the same thing, namely visibility obscured by water droplets in the air, with fog being the thicker of the two. Haze is due to solid particles.

Fog is caused by the surface temperature being colder than the air mass above it and so condensing the water vapour.

Fog found at sea is often advection fog, ie a transfer of conditions in a horizontal, as opposed to a vertical, plane of convection. Fog conditions occur as the air leaves the land; fog is therefore rarely found on windward coasts. The incidence of fog is also more likely with low wind speeds. Higher wind speeds cause fog to lift and form low stratus cloud.

Radiation fog may also affect waters surrounded largely by land. Land cools rapidly at night and the warm air rises and the land surface becomes chilled. Dawn is the worst time and this type of fog is most prevalent from autumn to spring.

Cold rising ocean currents are another cause of fog, the Grand Banks of Newfoundland being the area most famous for this.

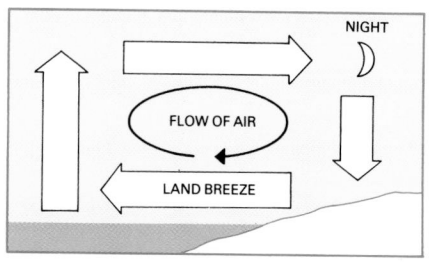

ABOVE *The flow of air which creates a land breeze. Because the land cools faster than the sea as night approaches, the air falls and moves over the water to take the place of air convected off the warmer sea, which in turn falls as it cools with height over the land.*

NAVIGATION

Understanding the basics of navigation is essential before venturing too far away from harbour. Although it is still far from a precise science, the responsible skipper and crew should be able to fix their position if visibility is suddenly reduced and establish if there will be enough water to return to the berth at the day's end.

EQUIPMENT

Charts are the prime source of information and these are available from the Hydrographic Department and their agents and chandlers. Charts must be kept up to date and a service is offered by chart agents although yachtsmen may do it themselves. For this they will need to study *Notices to Mariners*, regular booklets which convey information about lights being extinguished, buoys being moved and so on. Such charts and Notices are mostly produced with the needs of the professional seaman in mind. Commercial publishers also produce charts aimed specifically at the small boat market. Often they cover more convenient areas on the one sheet, or they may be presented in smaller, more convenient size.

Whichever charts you use, ensure that they are up-to-date. The choice of scale is important too. Scale determines the area covered and also the amount of detail included on the map. For passage making 1:150,000 is an acceptable scale; approaching a port or anchorage requires something in the order of 1:12,500.

The south coast of England, for example, is covered by 10 Admiralty charts in the 1:75,000 scale and they ought to be supplemented with larger scale harbour charts. It makes sense to stay with one style of chart as much as possible to avoid confusion with differing scales, abbreviations and symbols.

Charts are costly so it makes sense to buy no more than you will need to cover the area you intend to sail in. Keeping them up to date extends their life but do not make the false economy of having too few charts. Foul weather can force a change in the best prepared plans so you must make sure that your chart portfolio covers all potential 'bolt holes'.

Other essential publications include tide tables, which give the times and height of tides and a tidal stream atlas showing the flow direction and rate of the tide. You will also need a *List of Lights* and a *Radio List* for your sailing area. These tend to be expensive government publications so look out for almanacs which are amazingly good value. As compendiums, they are without match, combining information from many sources. Most almanacs offer a free amendment service so take advantage of them. It is inadvisable to use last year's almanac because a surprising amount of information is revised each year, from port entry signals to tidal data.

Another source of valuable information is the *Yachtsman's Pilot* which combines all the available information regarding harbours, passages, anchorages and so on, and distills it into a narrative written by yachtsmen for yachtsmen. Harbour approaches are often illustrated with yacht's eye views in photographic and sketch form to help the yachtsman assemble information into a three-dimensional picture. Most popular sailing areas are now well covered by *Pilots* published by cruising clubs, charter yacht operators and nautical publishing houses.

Another essential is the log book: either a special book or just a notebook you can prepare yourself. The object of the book is to record every piece of useful information. As a minimum, one page should record time, course required, course steered, log reading, speed, distance run since previous reading, wind speed and direction, and barometric pressure.

The facing page can contain narrative such as the time a tack was made, when a sail change took place and information gathered in advance such as weather

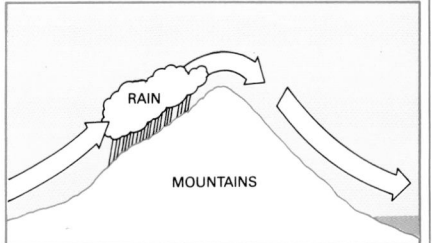

ABOVE *Katabatic winds. Such winds boost the land breeze. The air is forced up by the terrain, causing precipitation. Cooled by altitude, it rushes down out over the sea.* LEFT *The chart table must be easy to work at under sail.*

forecasts and tidal data. At any one time, there should be enough information contained in the log to work out the yacht's position.

All crew members should be encouraged to record information, while the narrative often provides entertaining reading about pleasures past. The log book is also a vital document of record. It may be required as evidence in a protest meeting after a race or to verify an insurance matter.

As regards equipment, chartwork will require soft pencils, a sharpener, rubber and brass dividers. The most practical type of dividers are those which can be used one-handed. For laying off courses parallel rules are sometimes used, but many small boat navigators much prefer easier-to-use plotters or protractors. The most common type uses a clear plastic square base with a rotating pointer arm used to plot and read courses or bearings. By aligning the base with the parallels and meridians marked on the chart the rotary arm can be swung to read the required course. Such simple use lends itself to cramped chart tables and the quick motion found in small yachts.

THE STEERING COMPASS

When matching the desired course heading on the floating compass card, think of the lubberline as the bow of the boat.

INSTRUMENTS

The single most important item is the steering compass. This should be easy to read with a clear card that's visible day and night. It should be gimballed and have corrector magnets to compensate for deviation on board the yacht caused by magnetic objects such as the auxiliary engine.

As the magnetic compass is used both to steer a course and show the heading which has been steered, it is vital that it should be set up parallel to the yacht's centreline. The card marked 0–360° floats in a spirit to damp its motion and readings are taken off reference lines called lubber lines.

Correcting deviation caused by local magnetic effects is a skilful job usually undertaken by a professional compass adjuster. Once a compass has been swung to find out the deviation two things can be done. Firstly, magnets within the compass can be used to minimize the effect. Secondly, when the effect has been reduced as much as possible, a table can be drawn up to show the remaining deviation on all headings. This can be converted into a graphical curve.

Once the compass has been swung, always be aware of deviation. Carelessness with knives, drinks cans, tape recorders can cause compass error, as can the fitting of additional equipment too close to the compass. Bad landfalls have been made because of the seemingly harmless can of beer enjoyed in the cockpit and put down too close by the compass. Cross check the main compass regularly with a hand bearing compass or the known bearing of fixed land objects.

Hand bearing compasses are used to take bearings of objects and are a vital element in position fixing. Modern hand bearers are light, cheap and easy to use. Because they are held close to the face, parallax error is eliminated.

Binoculars should also be carried aboard; vital for simple pilotage tasks such as spotting and reading buoys. The 7 × 50 is the most common type for sailing; 7 denotes the magnification power and 50 the size, in millimetres, of the front element. Although binoculars come in many combinations, 7 × 50 offer the attractive advantage of having well matched entry and exit pupils to allow maximum light to pass in poor conditions. The magnification power is not too great, making it possible to look at objects from a moving platform.

A more sophisticated aid is the echo sounder. In most coastal cruising, the nearest land is that directly underneath the keel, so these relatively cheap instruments are good value for navigation. You can buy an echo sounder reading to 325–490 ft (100–150 metres) with an alarm which can be set for shallow water, for less than the cost of a set of oilskins. Often there is a choice, in the cheaper ranges, between a flashing light display and a digital read-out. The former can be more useful because the strength of signal is shown, which may help to show up a returned signal from fish above the sea bed.

It will also pay to have a simple lead-line as a fail-safe back up. This can be used to cross-check the echo sounder. It can be used to 'feel' the bottom and check if an anchor is dragging, or loaded with grease, a lead line can bring up 'samples' of the bottom. When combined with a bearing, an accurate depth sounding can give a useful fix of your position. For this reason it is best to calibrate the instrument to show the actual depth of the water, not that under the keel or transducer, so remember that there will be less water under your keel than the echo sounder reads.

The log is another vital aid to fixing. By showing the distance run, a dead reckoning position can be calculated. Simple logs are trailed from the stern with a spinning rotator at the end of the line which transmits information onto the log's dial. More sophisticated electronic logs also show speed as well and work via through-hull transducers using devices such as miniature paddle wheels, Doppler effect sensors and ultrasonic sensors.

Unlike the trailing log, onboard electronic logs need careful calibration before use. A measured distance should be run two ways and the results calibrated for any tidal effects. The formula for this can be found in most almanacs.

ABOVE *The chart table is abandoned in favour of the Australian sunshine.*
LEFT *The hand bearing compass is a useful tool for position fixing.*

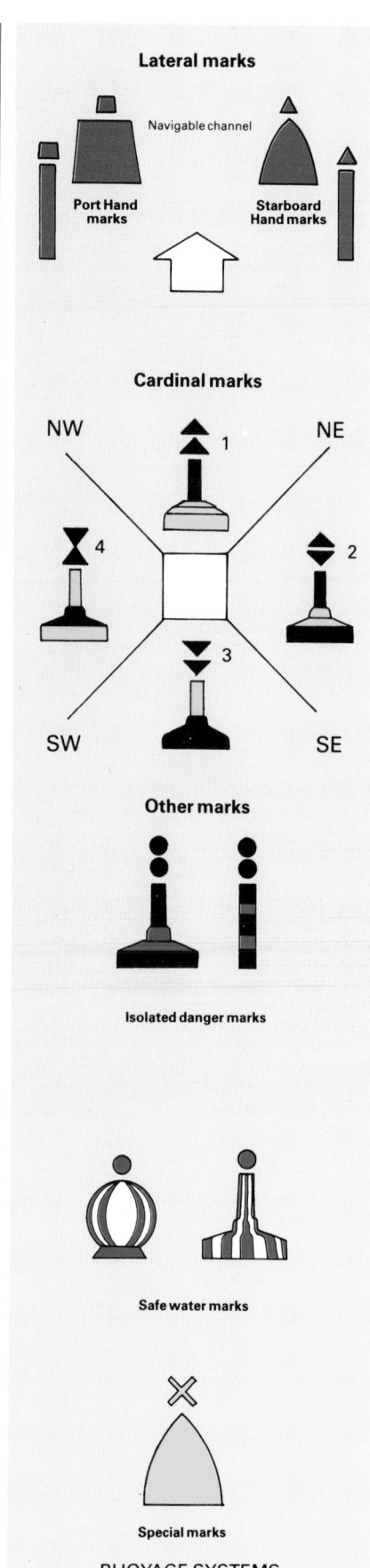

Lateral marks

Navigable channel

Port Hand marks

Starboard Hand marks

Cardinal marks

NW   1   NE

4

2

SW   3   SE

Other marks

Isolated danger marks

Safe water marks

Special marks

BUOYAGE SYSTEMS

MODERN ELECTRONIC AIDS

Until recently, RDF (Radio Direction Finding) was about the only electronic means to position fixing in poor visibility. But just as in home entertainment and computing generally, the microchip has brought a reduction in price and now position finders like Sat Nav, Decca and Loran are within reach of many boat owners.

Given the current pace of development we will undoubtedly see the electronic chart table within a few years. A computer visual display will show all chart functions while the computer will hold all almanac data and process information from performance indicators such as the log and integrate it with a variety of other functions ranging from wind speed and direction to the latest position obtained by satellite. It is quite conceivable that production yacht builders will have such systems on the extras list within a decade.

Until then we can choose one or a combination, of Sat Nav, Loran, Decca and RDF.

The latter takes bearing from land-based radio beacons. The great advantage of this system is that it is cheap and receivers can be self-powered from internal dry cell batteries. Great care must be taken in its use for the signal can be affected by influences on the yacht, such as rigging, guard rails, atmospheric and topographical conditions.

The shoreside beacons broadcast an identification signal and then a long dash on which a bearing is taken. Almanacs give full details of frequencies, times and identification codes.

Sat Nav gains positions from satellites originally placed in orbit for military applications. Yacht Sat Navs now require far less power than early units and will give fixes of great accuracy virtually anywhere in the world. A fix is updated each time a satellite passes overhead; some areas are better served than others. In between fixes the instrument uses yacht speed and course data to give an estimated position, usually shown in latitude and longitude.

In planning a cruise or the course of a race, points along the way (way points) can be keyed into the instrument. This allows it to give you a course and distance from one way point to the next.

Decca and Loran (Long Range Navigation Aid) offer much the same with two important differences. One is that they rely on continuously broadcast signals so that fixes are constantly upgraded. This may make them a better choice in coastal waters. Secondly, because they rely on ground stations, their usefulness is limited to areas where such aerials are placed. Loran is particularly strong in North America and the Mediterranean, while Decca coverage is found in north west Europe and other areas used heavily by commercial shipping. Both devices also allow way points to be keyed in.

THE CHART TABLE

No matter how elementary or sophisticated your instrumentation, you ought to have an efficient work station. Even small yachts usually have a chart table. If not, it is possible to work on the saloon table, in the cockpit or on a special plotting board resting on your knees. The key is organization: sensibly sited instruments, almanacs, dividers, rules and pencils to hand; and thorough preparation and research of tidal data, buoys, lights etc.

Navigation is about the elimination of error and making valued assessments of information. A methodical method and tidy work place help enormously.

Ideally, the chart table should be usable in all conditions and dry no matter how foul the outside conditions. Wet charts and drowned electronics can be a step on a yacht's road to tragedy, as errors, inefficiencies and circumstances compound into a total picture potentially more dangerous than any of the individual problems.

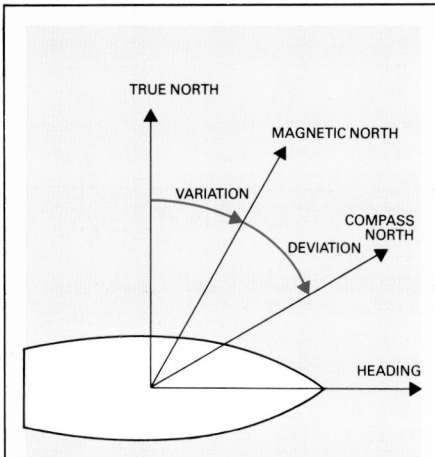

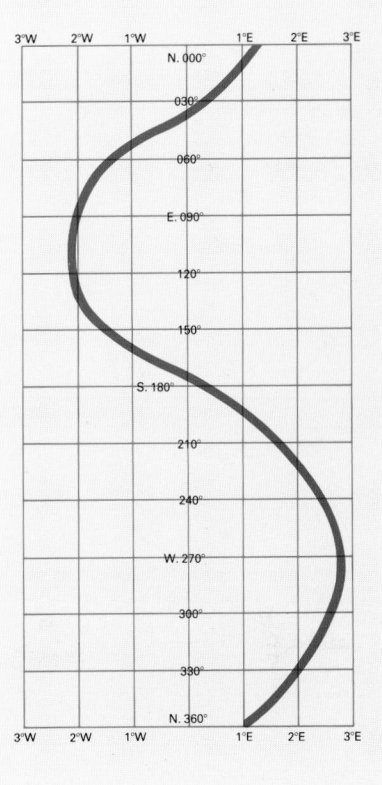

ABOVE *The curve shows compass deviation, an interesting alternative to the more conventional deviation card with its list of numbers.*

LEFT *A marker buoy with a radar reflector.*

FAR LEFT *Buoyage systems; lateral marks are generally used to indicate the sides of well defined navigable channels. Port hand light is red, starboard is green or white. Cardinal marks indicate the direction from the mark in which the best navigable water lies. They also show bends or forks in the channel. Their white lights flash as follows: 1 very quick or quick. 2 Three flashes every five or ten seconds. 3 Six flashes plus a longer flash every ten to fifteen seconds. 4 Nine flashes every ten or fifteen seconds. Danger marks have two flashing white lights. Safe water marks are in mid-channel or indicate a landfall, with isophased white lights or one long flash every ten seconds. Other marks use a yellow light. For the significance of shapes and colours, consult the International Regulations for Collisions at Sea.*

NAVIGATION – NORTH

The navigator will use three 'Norths'. True North is determined by the meridians. Magnetic North is found after an allowance has been made for the earth's magnetic field. Compass North is found after applying deviation to the yacht's own compass caused by metallic objects on board.

SAIL THEORY

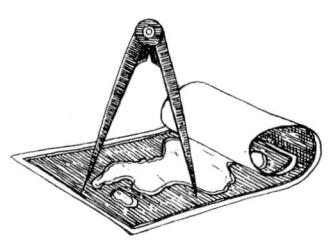

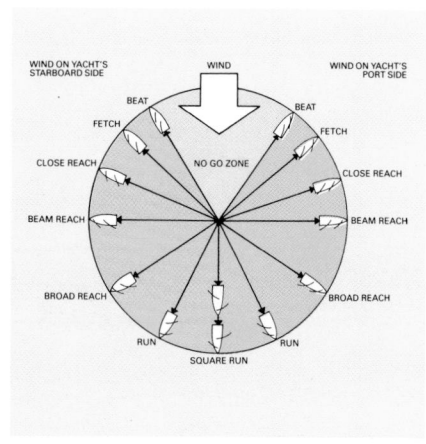

ABOVE *Points of sailing.*
OPPOSITE *The slot between mainsail and jib.*

A sailing boat moves through two different mediums at once; the hull through water and the sails through air. Both components are complementary – a sailing boat moves efficiently if her hull is well designed, clean and fair, and if her well-cut sails are correctly set. Good sails are not enough to transform a slow old hull on their own. There is no point having the raciest looking yacht and equipment if they are not correctly used.

The principal points of sailing are beating, reaching and running. Fortunately they are very colourful terms and are easy to remember. You beat into the wind. You reach across it. You run away from it.

In between, there are other points of sailing such as a close reach and broad reach, points of sail in fact all around the clock, except one – directly into the wind.

Sailing away from the wind is the easiest for the newcomer to understand. Everything we know in everyday life is blown away from the wind, be it leaves on the ground or clouds in the sky.

We call this running away, with the wind pushing the yacht ahead of itself. To catch the wind it is logical that the maximum sail be presented to the wind, so the sheets are eased and out go the sails.

SAILING UPWIND

Flow across the sails is vital for upwind sailing since they are used to generate aerodynamic lift. Again, everyday objects can aid our understanding of lift. If we hold an umbrella upright in a wind it will try and lift out of our hand. This is because the air flowing over the top of the curved crown has to travel further and is accelerated. This decreases the pressure on the upper surface and the suction effect produced is called lift.

An aircraft wing works on the same principle. The top surface is curved while the underside is much flatter. The accelerated airflow over the top side produces the necessary lift. When more lift is required for takeoff (or landing because speed is reduced), flaps on both the leading and trailing edges of the wing increase the curve so accentuating the faster flow on the top of the wing and decelerating the flow on the underside.

This is why sailing craft cannot sail straight into the wind. The airflow has to strike the sail at an angle so that it flows over a curved lifting surface. Approximately 45° is as close as a yacht can go into the wind, although some really efficient upwind boats such as America's Cup twelve metre yachts can go closer.

This lift converts into forward propulsion owing to the interaction between rig and hull. When the wind strikes the sail it is redirected aft. This causes a movement just as would be the case if you were to hold your hand out of the window of a moving car: slant the hand upwards and you deflect the flow of air, with the result that your hand is forced to rise.

This follows Newton's law that every action has an equal and opposite reaction. Thus wind moving across the sails produces a sideways and forward

force. If the sideways force can be countered, the forward component predominates. Hence the yacht sails forward.

Imagine a triangular block: if something is placed behind it, to resist sideways movement, then by applying a force (wind) to the angled side of the block (sails) the block is squeezed forward.

THE SLOT

On a yacht there are usually two sails working in harness: the mainsail and the headsail, or jib. Their total area as well as the interaction between them combine to make an efficient propulsion system.

The gap between the main and the jib is known as the slot and it allows the total thrust of main and jib combined to be greater than the sum of the thrust of each individual sail.

Tests conducted in the wind tunnel have shown that aerofoils are more efficient when a slot is introduced because it helps guide the flow of air across the back, or leeward, side of the foil. For maximum effect the back of the jib should be level with the point of the mainsail's maximum power, the fullest part of its sectional shape.

If the slot is too narrow, the air is literally choked as it tries to pass through the constriction. The evidence for this is backwinding on the mainsail.

Similarly, a slot can be too wide and the air coming through will be turbulent, instead of the clean, attached flow which is being sought.

TRUE AND APPARENT WIND

Sailors are very wind-conscious and are aware that there are two types of wind to be understood.

The first is the true wind which literally means the wind which is unaffected by other influences in terms of direction and velocity.

The second is the apparent wind which has been affected by some other factor. Basically, it is the sailing vessel's own movement which causes the true wind to be modified into the apparent wind. Therefore it is the apparent wind which determines which sails are to be set and how they are to be trimmed.

Burgees at the masthead and even electronic wind indicators with their cups and vanes show apparent wind. It is only the more sophisticated instruments that can integrate apparent wind speed and direction with the yacht's heading and speed and so can resolve the true wind speed calculation.

When beating upwind therefore, it follows that the apparent wind is stronger than the true one. This is because the apparent wind is the true wind speed plus that of the yacht moving towards it. Moreover, not only does the wind appear to increase in strength but its direction moves forward also.

When sailing downwind the opposite applies. The apparent wind is less than the true wind speed because the yacht is moving in the same direction and consequently, its own speed can be subtracted. The inexperienced sailor can be fooled into underestimating or overestimating the true wind speed by the yacht's own movement.

This difference between true and apparent wind speed should of course determine how much sail is set. Starting off on a downwind course it is easy to be lulled into thinking how pleasant a moderate fresh breeze can be. With full sail set, the yacht will be bowling along until it is time to head for home. Then the yacht heels over, cups and kettles crash around below and oilskins are suddenly necessary.

With careful thought this need not happen. The sail plan should be reduced with a reef in the mainsail and a smaller jib set, making the upwind leg as enjoyable as the downwind one.

WINCHING

For efficiency, one person winds the winch while another tails the sheet.

OPPOSITE *Looking through the slot; with correct sail trim, it is the slot effect which generates real drive.*

ABOVE *The slot is a 'venturi' or a narrowing of space through which a liquid or gas – in this case air – is forced. For maximum effect, note that the back of the jib is level with the point of the mainsail's maximum power.*
FAR RIGHT TOP *When the yacht heels it becomes overpressed and unbalanced. Here the helmsman is experiencing weather helm.*
FAR RIGHT *The narrower the slot the faster the air flow. 1 Correct setting. 2 Narrower for light airs. 3 Choked.*

HEEL AND STABILITY

A yacht is able to sail upwind because the side force is resisted by the keel and hull form of the vessel. But because the hull is streamlined for forward motion the yacht moves along the least line of resistance. What side force remains has to be spent somehow and this results in heeling.

A parallelogram of forces is at work when a boat sails. Upwind the side force is considerable with relatively little forward drive. On a reach, both side force and forward drive move towards the direction of the yacht's travel. The effect is even more pronounced on a broad reach. This is why a broad reach is the fastest point of sailing, because all the forces slant towards the yacht's heading and side force is minimal. In a dinghy for instance, the centreboard would be raised as its resistance is scarcely required.

How much a yacht heels as a result of these forces depends both on the hull shape and its ballasting. As far as hull shape is concerned, beam is the major factor. Following the popularity of racing yachts designed to the International

Offshore Rule, beamy boats are now common. Beam produces lots of space below decks while offering stability which consequently requires less ballast and hence less cost to the builder.

Form stability is derived from the shape of the hull alone. Its effect is quite pronounced at low angles of heel but as the angle increases so too does the effect of the ballast.

Thus the lower the ballast and the greater its amount, the greater the stability a yacht will have. Too much too low, however, is not the ideal answer, for it produces an uncomfortable pendulum-like motion. As in all aspects of yacht design, the best solution is a careful trade-off among many factors.

The resistance to heel is known as stiffness. Any yacht of reasonable beam with a high ballast ratio (ie the ballast forms a high proportion of the vessel's total weight) will be stiff, whereas a shallow-hulled yacht with internal ballast (common in many racing yachts) coupled with only moderate ballast in the keel and perhaps a large sail plan, would be considered tender.

HULL FORM AND SAIL BALANCE

The way hull shape and sail area interact has much to do with a yacht's behaviour. This is often referred to as balance, and to sail both fast and comfortably both the hull and sail plan need to be trimmed carefully.

Hull balance is a function of the yacht's form. A heeled yacht will behave differently to an upright yacht. The greater the difference between the bow and stern shapes, the more pronounced this difference will be. A modern yacht with its characteristic fine bow and full wide stern can be difficult to handle if it is allowed to heel too far for it will want to turn into the wind. Moreover, the forward force applied to the sails will no longer be above the centreline of the yacht but out to the leeward side.

So while an older style yacht with narrow beam and long matching overhangs may be more balanced at high angles of heel, the modern yacht offers a winning combination of space and performance.

The effect of any imbalance is felt through the helm. As the yacht tries to steer itself into the wind, so the helmsman will have to apply increasing resistance to the pull of the helm. This load on the helm is called weather helm. Some amount of weather helm is desirable. If the helm is left unattended, most yachts ought to sail slowly into the wind until the wind spills from their sails. Thereafter they will lie almost stationary to one side of the wind or other. This is similar to most yachts' behaviour when no sails are set: most will lie beam onto the wind or lie stern first:

Weather helm can also be induced by the sail plan. The most common reason is too much sail being carried which just overpowers the yacht. The cause may also be such fundamental design errors as the mast being stepped too far forward or the sail plan not being of the right proportions. The mast may have been stepped with too much rake aft.

Lee helm is the opposite of weather helm, ie the yacht's tendency to bear away unless checked by the tiller or wheel. Again there could be something wrong with the design but this is rare. If the yacht has a fractional rig this may cause lee helm. This means she has a large mainsail area and smaller foretriangle. When reefed down, the mainsail may be such a small proportion of its normal area that the balance of the boat is upset.

More commonly lee helm is found in light airs. The helmsman might find the yacht difficult to steer because the helm is vague and lacking feel. More bite can be obtained by heeling the yacht to leeward, so that it goes into a state of slight imbalance owing to the assymetric hull shape. This, we know now, makes the yacht want to turn into the wind, so giving the helm the feel the helmsman is striving for.

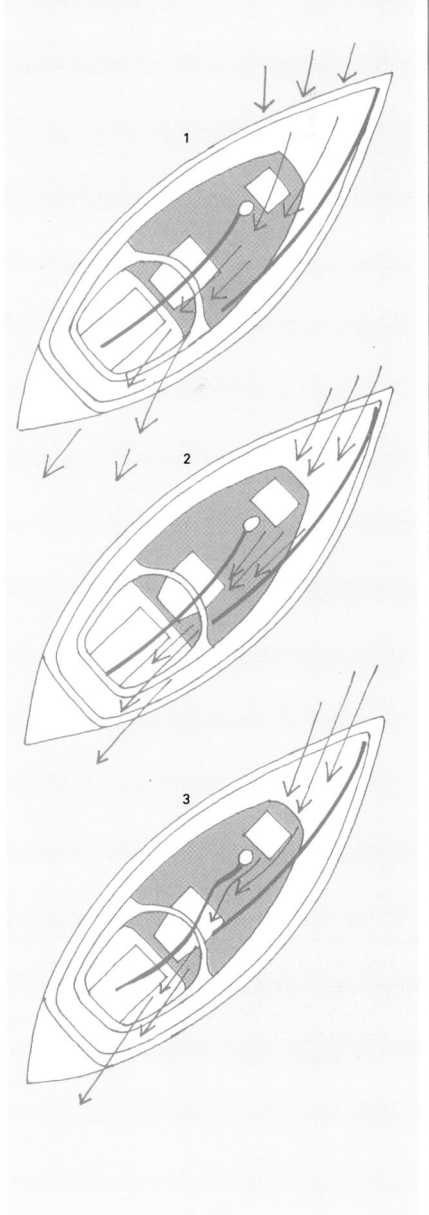

CHAPTER FIVE

ENGINES AND AUXILIARIES

Successful handling under power demands an understanding of your yacht's auxiliary installation, the vessel's behaviour and the ability to apply this knowledge while taking into account variable wind and water conditions.

A thorough understanding of handling under power is vital for the beginner because most of the trickier manoeuvres will be carried out in this way as confidence is gained in boat-handling. Modern yachts handle exceptionally well under power and there is not much to be gained by tackling close quarters situations under sail.

Today, most engines are small efficient diesels with enough power to move the yacht at her theoretical maximum speed in flat water and to punch against a foul tide and/or a head sea in unfavourable conditions. This power, combined with the current practice of short keels and separate rudders allows the modern yacht to turn in its own length and accelerate and stop with ease, something which could never be said about the old generation of long-keeled yachts.

Diesel engines are now smaller, lighter and more powerful than ever before. Their reliability is commendable, given the hostile environment in which they operate and engine makers are now making greater efforts to mount service points such as pumps, dipsticks and filters at the front of the engine to make maintenance easier.

A typical engine will be sited in an enclosed space under the cockpit companionway area, preferably insulated with sound absorbent material. To give the engine ventilation, trunking will draw air in from outside, preferably assisted by a spark-proof fan. Fuel is brought from the remote tank, often by copper piping and wire-cased flexible hosing. There should be a stopcock on the tank which in turn needs to be electrically earthed against static electricity. Because marine fuel is often dirty a filter must be fitted for debris and a water trap for condensate.

Raw sea water is drawn in either to cool the engine directly itself or the intercooler which has a recirculating fresh water cooling system. Seacocks are fitted to both inlet and outlet. The exhaust is vented to the outside. Sometimes cooling water is added to help silence and cool the exhaust and a water trap is fitted to the system to prevent such water running back to the engine when the yacht heels.

TYPE OF DRIVE

The engine's power is delivered to the propeller via a shaft. The shaft takes its power from the reduction gearbox and passes through the hull via a stern tube and gland. This can be water- or grease-lubricated. The engine can be mounted back-to-front and the drive arranged in a Vee formation.

The most novel and space-efficient system is the saildrive, developed by Volvo of Sweden 10 years ago and widely copied since. Here the engine is mounted in its own beds glassed into the hull (as opposed to being fitted to the yacht's structure via flexible mountings) and the drive passes through a neoprene membrane in the hull to an outboard-style leg. Such a system is very

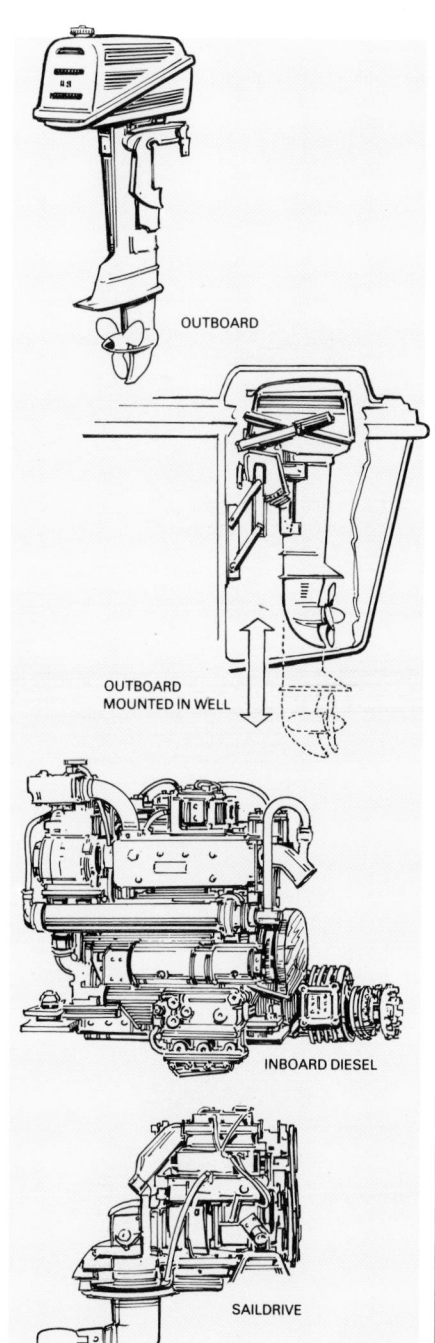

OUTBOARD

OUTBOARD MOUNTED IN WELL

INBOARD DIESEL

SAILDRIVE

ABOVE *Types of engines.*
OPPOSITE *A massive diesel undergoes a performance test; the engine belongs to a 100 footer (30 m).*

SEACOCKS

Seacocks pass through the hull. They must therefore be accessible in case of failure.

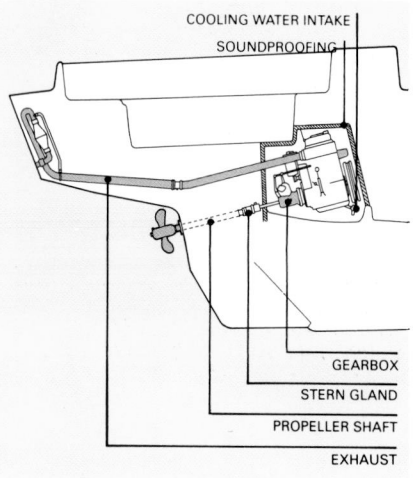

COOLING WATER INTAKE
SOUNDPROOFING

GEARBOX
STERN GLAND
PROPELLER SHAFT
EXHAUST

ABOVE *Typical inboard installation.*

compact and does away with the need for careful alignment of shaft, sterngear and engine. Fears about membrane failure have so far proven groundless and other engine builders, such as Bukh of Denmark, fit a double membrane with a water alarm in between.

OUTBOARD ENGINES

While inboard engines are common in yachts over 25ft (8m), outboard engines offer a cheap alternative below that length and are much cheaper to buy and easier to maintain.

They do use more fuel however; often a smelly two-stroke oil/petrol mixture. Again, engine manufacturers have improved outboards for sailing yachts – four stroke engines and special lower revving units are available, turning a much coarser-bladed propeller, which is more suitable to the task of pushing a yacht along as opposed to a small, light day boat. Controls are front mounted, and a particularly useful option is a power take-off and battery charging facility.

Many small yachts mount their outboards on a sliding/hingeing bracket on the transom. This is far from satisfactory; the engine lifts clear of the water in a sea or with the crew on the foredeck; it requires awkward leaning and lifting over the transom; fuel caps and engine cowlings can be accidentally dropped.

Much better are those which drive the yacht through an opening in the hull surrounded by a well, especially if all the controls are close by the helm.

CONTROLS

Clearly it is easier if the engine controls fall readily to hand. It can be awkward for the helmsman to reach the throttle and gearshift of outboard engines mounted on the transom.

A single lever usually controls the ahead-neutral-astern gearshift and throttle in one arc of movement. Such levers should be within easy reach, yet shielded against accidental snagging by feet or oilskin trousers. Larger yachts with wheel steering can have the engine controls mounted on the steering pedestal – a real convenience.

In sight should be an engine rev counter, fuel gauge and water temperature gauge/alarm. The latter gives early warning of a blocked engine-cooling water intake. It is also most helpful if the engine can be started up and shut down from the cockpit: the engine may be required in an instant.

PROPELLERS

Propellers in water work in just the same way as their counterparts do in air; their foil-shaped blades create lift. Generally the slower the speed of the shaft the larger the blades can be. Compare the relatively slow turning two-bladed propeller fitted to a yacht auxiliary engine to the fast turning three-bladed propeller found on a high power outboard engine. Reduction gearboxes are often fitted to inboard engines for this reason.

Having the right propeller is important for getting maximum drive, especially as engine performance can be reduced by factors such as friction losses, power take-off for alternators, low energy value fuel or high operating temperatures.

For the sailing yacht, there is a complicated trade-off between drag and efficiency. Cruising yachts will have large fixed two- or three-bladed propellers. Racing yachts will have two-bladed propellers which either fold closed or feather in line with the water flow.

Perhaps the ideal solution is a controllable-pitch feathering propeller. Drag is reduced whilst sailing and when the engine is used, the propeller pitch can be

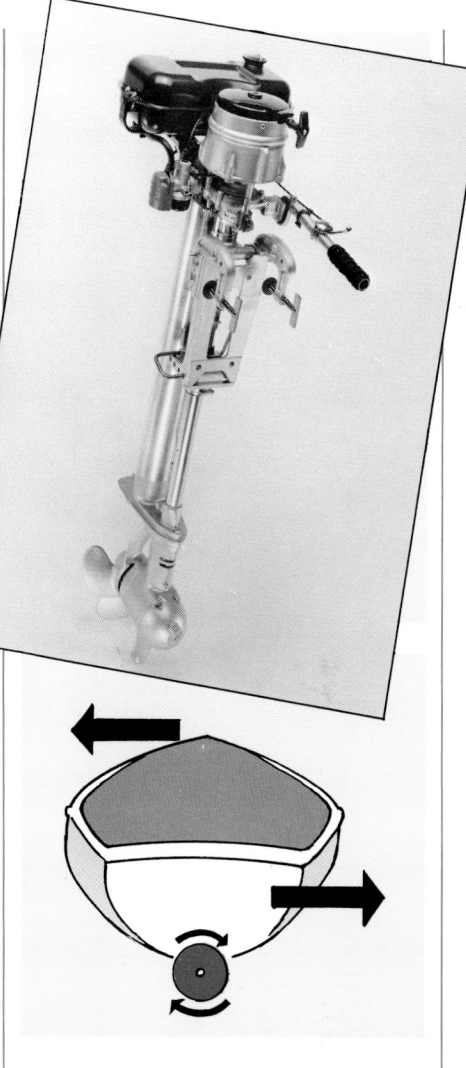

matched to the engine revs to give maximum speed and economy. Such propellers are, however, expensive.

The propeller has a marked effect on the handling of the yacht because of the propeller or 'paddlewheel' effect. Here the propeller literally paddles the vessel in the direction of its rotation. Hence a clockwise or right-handed propeller (when viewed from astern) will move the boat to the right while an anticlockwise, or left-handed, propeller will move the vessel to the left.

For this reason, most yachts have a tighter turning circle one way than the other. A right-handed propeller will move the stern to starboard, swing the bows to port and tighten the turn in that direction.

The effect is even more noticeable when going astern, so much so that some yachts may be unable to steer 'against' the propeller. The answer here, is to give a burst of power to get the yacht moving astern and then back off the power so allowing the rudder to work unhindered.

THE RUDDER

The better the water flow over the rudder blade the more effective it is. The ideal configuration for ease of handling is the relatively short keel and propeller mounted ahead of the rudder pushing water past it. If the boat is light and doesn't have excessive freeboard and windage she should handle like a dream.

The turning effect of the rudder is accentuated by the shape of the yacht when she turns, because the water will pass either side of the hull at different pressure, so forcing the bow around faster still.

Yachts don't turn around their mid points; instead, they pivot roughly one third of the way aft from the bow when going forwards. This is a characteristic to be aware of, for while you are concentrating on clearing the bow around an obstacle, the stern could be arcing in towards another.

Applying more rudder is not necessarily the way to tighten a turn. If you apply more than approximately 30° of helm the water flow is disturbed so much that the rudder acts more as a brake.

When going astern, the load on the rudder is much greater. Going ahead, the rudder is suspended in the water from its hangings; while going astern it is the 'wrong' way around. A firm hand is needed to prevent the blade being forced to one side or the other, stressing the pintles and steering gear. The rudder in this situation is like a weather vane pointing upwind – the wind is trying to force it around to lie downwind.

TOP LEFT *An outboard engine mounted on the transom.*
TOP RIGHT *A long shaft outboard (5 hp), suitable for the 16 to 22 ft (5 to 7 m) boat.*
ABOVE *The 'paddlewheel effect'.*

CHAPTER SIX

BOAT HANDLING

Prior assessment of the situation and consideration of every alternative action is the key to successful boat handling. Combine this with confidence, a thorough knowledge of your yacht's handling characteristics and a well-briefed crew, then manoeuvring in close quarters should be fairly straightforward.

Everyone who has spent time in boats knows that nothing always goes according to plan, so the seamanlike sailor will not get himself into dead-end situations. He will also not be too proud to abort an approach and have another go. Indeed, the knowledge gained on the first run could lead to a more elegant solution, rather than a clumsy piece of boat handling where one error is compounded by the next.

WIND AND TIDE

Almost every situation will be influenced to some degree by the wind and/or the tide, thus being aware of which factor exerts the greatest influence will determine your course of action. As a general rule, it is easiest to depart or arrive with bow facing whichever is the strongest – the wind or tide – because the yacht will handle more precisely that way.

You should already know from your preparation what the tide state will be at a given time and the direction of the prevailing wind. For close quarters manoeuvring, check for other visual clues: flags or smoke ashore will tell you about the wind; burgees or masthead wind vanes on nearby yachts will show if there are eddies or a blanketing effect; buoys and pontoons will show how much tide there is streaming past the point you wish to make fast to.

COMMUNICATION

When the helmsman has planned his course of action he should brief the crew. They will need to know where the yacht is going, what warps are required and on which side they and the fenders should be made ready.

For their part the crew should query anything they feel unsure of or pass on any information the skipper may have missed, such as seeing a yacht preparing to leave close by the destination.

The crew should prepare the fenders and warps. If the sails are being dropped they should be stowed to prevent them obscuring the helmsman's view or from being lost over the side. However, do not de-rig them completely if you are approaching under sail. Leave the halyard bent on so that by loosening a few sail ties you can hoist again should the engine fail.

As for the warps they should be both strong and twice the boat length. The crew will make them up on cleats or bollards and pass them out through the pulpit or stern rail so that they run ashore directly. The remaining warp should be coiled or flaked out on deck in a zig-zag pattern. If you intend to pass a line to another person ashore or onboard another yacht, make a loop with a bowline in the end to be passed ashore, so that it can be slipped instantly over a cleat or bollard, allowing you to adjust the warp to the correct length from onboard.

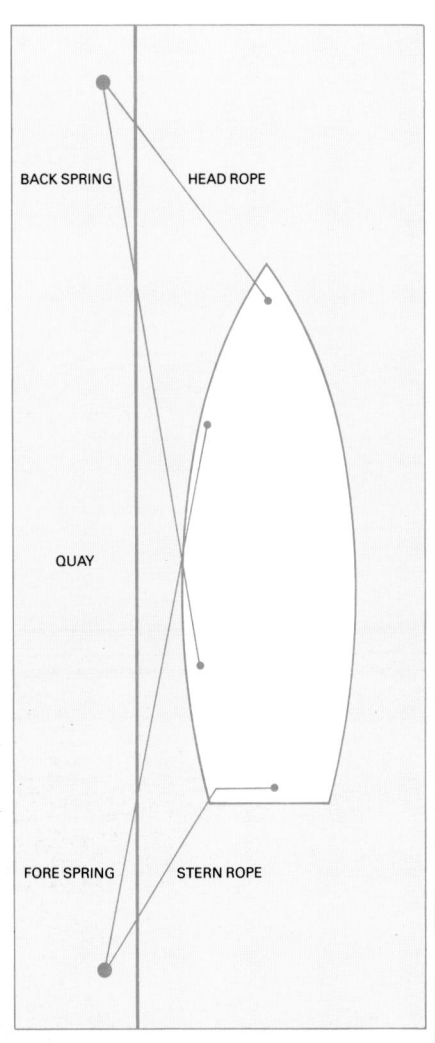

ABOVE *The nomenclature and positioning of warps.*
OPPOSITE *The spinnaker and extra sail area are set for downwind sailing.*

Make sure everybody knows how to throw a line so as to avoid the all-too-frequent comic scene of a line landing short of the target in a tangled mess.

The rope should be coiled in even loops in a clockwise direction (because of the way rope is constructed in a spiral twist) adding a clockwise twist to ensure each loop lies flat against the previous one. Always recoil a warp as a previously coiled one can easily become tangled if just one loop slips inside another. Divide the completed coil in two, with slightly less than half held in your throwing hand. Then, standing side-on to the target, swing the coil in a smooth underarm arc to a point higher than the target. The remaining warp should pay out freely from your other hand.

It is important to remember that a yacht is always on the move, so securing the yacht in a logical order is vital. With the bow pointing uptide or upwind, it is clearly vital to get the bow line ashore first and secured, to prevent the bow shearing off. If you are shorthanded, the bow line and stern spring can be taken ashore together by one crewman, which provides control of both bow and stern until they can be secured and the remaining lines made fast.

It might be necessary to stop the boat with warps, if approaching downwind or downtide. Here the stern line (if the yacht is making headway), or even better a line from a cleat amidships, should be taken ashore, and a turn taken around cleat or bollard. As the load comes on the line, it should be eased out to brake the yacht. There is no point in leaping ashore, cleating off the line and expecting the yacht to stop dead as soon as the warp goes taut. Even a small yacht can displace over one ton and will have considerable momentum. A crash stop is likely to damage the fitting to which the warp is attached.

MOORINGS

There really should be little problem with picking and leaving a mooring. The helmsman's control of speed and direction will dictate success or failure.

It helps if you aim slightly uptide or upwind of the buoy so that as you slow the yacht drift will be towards the buoy, not away from it. A look at other moored yachts will show if they are wind-rode (ie lying into the wind) or tide-rode (lying into the tide); look for a similar type of vessel. A motor yacht with high superstructure will be more affected by the wind than a heavy yacht with a deep keel, for example. Prearranged signals with the crewman forward can be used to indicate speed and direction requirements.

When approaching under sail, the most favourable line will be on a beam reach under mainsail alone. This keeps the jib out of the way of the foredeck while the reaching course allows plenty of scope for altering course up and downwind without having to tack or gybe – something best avoided in crowded moorings.

A beam reach also gives good speed control. The sails can be eased to slow and stop the yacht, or sheeted in for more power. Experience will tell you when to turn into the wind for the final approach, though a rule of thumb is approximately two boatlengths.

You may need to approach under headsail, when downwind but uptide. By using the jib and not the mainsail you can spill wind by letting the jib flap, whereas the mainsail would be prevented from going right out by the shrouds. Make sure the jib sheets are eased right out as you reach to the buoy so that you don't sail over it. The jib can be dropped as soon as the yacht is made fast.

Often however, the wind and tide neither conveniently stream the same way nor in direct opposition, but rather slant across each other. The same rules apply though: use the mainsail with the wind ahead and the jib for a stern wind.

To leave a mooring, the reverse applies. To make sure that the yacht pays off onto the correct tack if you are sailing, or to clear the mooring rope from the propeller if using the engine, walk aft down the side deck holding the mooring or pick-up buoy to turn the yacht to the desired direction.

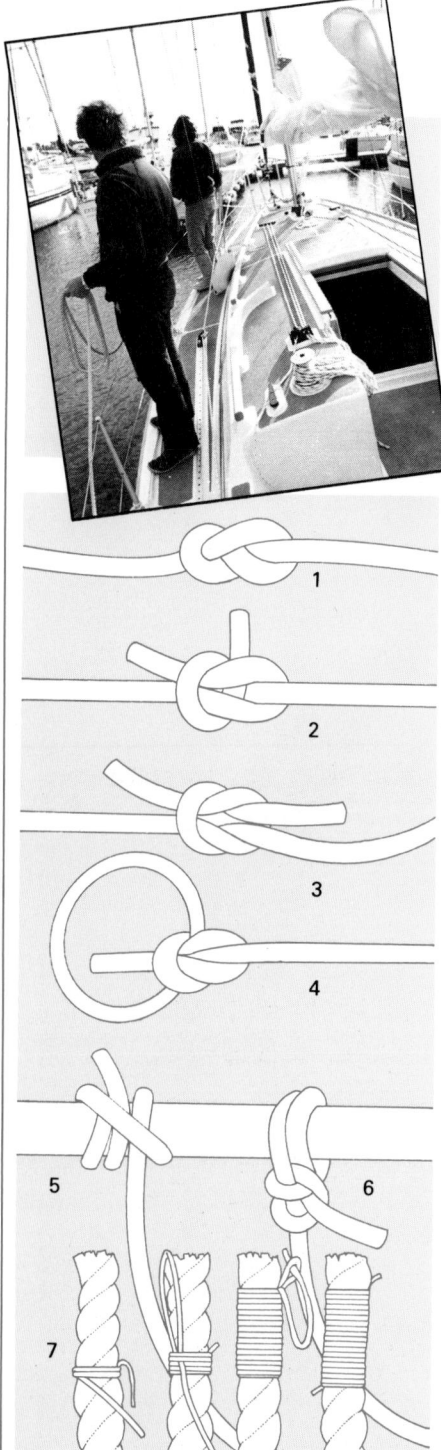

ABOVE *Ropework is still a way of life for the sailor; even those yachtsmen and women who opt for the protected waters of inshore sailing need to be able to handle elementary knots and rope splicing. 1 A figure of eight, used to stop a rope slipping through an eye or block. 2 A sheet bend, for joining two ropes of unequal thickness or fastening a line to an eye. 3 A reef knot, originally used to tie reefing lines. 4 The bowline forms an eye at the end of the rope. 5 A rolling hitch, for tying a rope to a spar. 6 A round turn and two half hitches, often used to tie a rope to any standing object. 7 Whipping, or finishing the ends of rope with twine to prevent them unravelling.*

PILE MOORINGS

Unless there is no alternative, these are best tackled under power rather than sail. Again, assess whether wind or tide is strongest and plan an approach in the relevant direction. The aim with pile moorings is to attach both a bow line and a stern line.

If the wind and tide are from the same direction you should be able to nose the bow towards the upwind/uptide pile so that the bow line can be attached. Then you can drop back, secure the stern line and adjust both lines until the yacht is equidistant between the two.

When wind and tide are opposed, steer into the stronger of the two and attach the stern line first. Then it should be paid out as the yacht moves forward, to attach the bow line. This is known as a running moor because you secure the warp as you pass the pile. Clearly, the warp must be tended throughout the moor to stop it fouling the propeller.

The same system is used if the wind and tide are at right angles. Invariably the wind will be on the beam and the piles are laid in line with the tide, so after attaching the stern line, steer upwind of the forward pile to attach the bow line.

Because control of the yacht is so vital, attempting this undersail is not recommended. It could be better to consider other options. You might try just treating one pile as a mooring and thus make sure of getting a bow line secure. Then take a stern line out to the other pile with the tender. Or if another yacht is lying between the piles, go in alongside her and rig your lines as quickly as possible to ensure the other yacht's lines are not unduly overstrained.

To leave pile moorings you will need to double up your lines so that they can be slipped. This means passing them through the ring and bringing the bitter-end back on board. The benefit of two really long warps will become obvious as joined warps will not run through the ring easily. When you are ready to go, slip the line under the least load first so that the remaining warp keeps the yacht facing into the wind and tide.

If you are alongside another yacht, the bow and stern lines can be recovered by the tender and then you can depart normally.

Instead of piles, some harbours or rivers might have fore-and-aft buoys laid and they can be tackled the same way.

MARINA BERTHS

Because berthing density is so great in a marina, some operators insist that yachts enter and leave only under power. Because space is so tight the simple marina berth may require quite complex manoeuvres, especially if your yacht does not handle well astern, Or if there is no space to turn normally.

Strong winds or fast running tides cause the majority of problems in marinas, preventing the yacht turning fast enough or pinning it against the pontoon.

In most circumstances it should be possible to turn into the berth and have the crew step neatly ashore with the warps. If the wind or tide is taking the yacht away from the berth, steer at it, and straighten her up at the last moment. When leaving, a gentle push off the pontoon and a burst of power should do the trick.

If, when you want to leave, the wind or tide is pinning the yacht against the pontoon, it is likely that the bow won't swing sufficiently towards wind or tide for the yacht to turn. In these circumstances, slip all the lines except the stern spring. Then walk the yacht or gently motor astern until the berth is almost cleared. Take the weight on the spring, and the yacht will use it as a fulcrum. But watch the bows: they will swing in a wide arc and might not clear the opposite pontoon or neighbouring yacht, without the spring being used again.

Alternatively, just keeping the bow line tight after the others have been cast off may be enough to swing the yacht off the berth and for her to motor clear.

Some marinas have yachts lying stern-to rather than alongside a finger

FAR LEFT TOP *The crew make ready with the dock lines for a marina berth.*
TOP *Pile moorings in Australia.*
ABOVE *Moored bows-to. With no significant wind or tide and plenty of space available, manoeuvring in or out should present little difficulty under power.*

ABOVE *Rafting up: fenders must be adjusted to a suitable height.*
RIGHT *Moored bow-and stern-to in Yugoslavia.*

pontoon. Securing the bow will be either a pair of piles to which warps are attached or a mooring buoy attached to a ground chain or weight under water. If you use such a marina, you will find the step-through style of pulpit or stern boarding ladder arrangement of real benefit.

If there is no significant wind or tide the yacht can be steered in either bow or stern first. Control the speed so that the crew can put a line over the pile or attach it to a ring on it. In the case of a mooring, the buoy will have to be picked up with a boat hook. Then motor towards the quay so that the shore lines from either side of the yacht can be made fast; the weight of all lines pulling against each other will hold the yacht clear of the quay.

If you lie stern-to it might help to cross the stern lines so that they act like springs. As a general rule, the more a warp can act at an acute angle to the yacht, the more it is able to hold it in a given position.

If you have a regular berth, arrange permanent dock lines attached to the piles which can be hung on a hook on each pile. Then, you should be able to simply reach out for them at a convenient height, rather then fish for them in the water with a boat hook.

When a cross-wind or tide is present, be sure to allow for drift and aim to secure the uptide/upwind warps first. Similarly, when leaving, these lines should be last to be slipped.

ANCHORING STERN-TO

Much of the above holds true when anchoring stern- or bow-to. The former is preferable, for the anchor gear is at the bow, making it easier to set and recover. By cross springing the stern, the yacht will also be more stationary on the quay.

If there is cross-wind or side tide, lay the anchor into it to allow the yacht to drift down into her berth.

In a harbour, the depth of water should not be great, so the anchor can be dropped about three boat lengths off the quay. Look at the angle made by the cables of neighbouring yachts and try not to let go your cable on top of them.

If the bow blows off-line as you reverse towards the quay, ask the crew to snub the anchor cable to straighten the yacht up. They can also brake the yacht as she comes up to the quay by the same method.

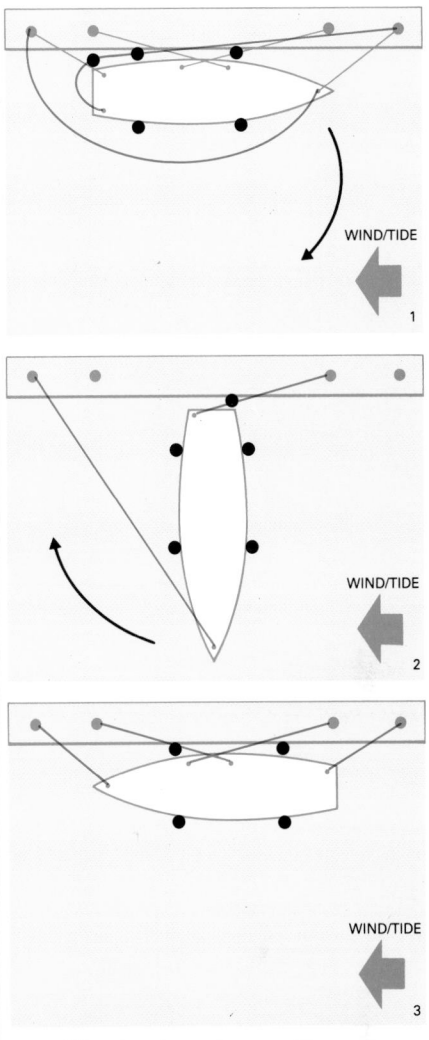

MOORING ALONGSIDE

Making fast alongside a quay, pontoon or jetty is probably the most common boat handling situation a skipper is likely to face.

As before, approaches under power are preferable. If the wind and tide are parallel to the shore make your approach into the stronger to ensure maximum control.

If the wind is onshore you can slow and stop the boat just off the quay and be blown, even into very tight spaces, by letting the wind drift the yacht in. In an offshore breeze, steer in at a more acute angle, straightening up at the last moment and making sure both bow and stern lines are made fast quickly.

When approaching under sail, look for the largest gap to give yourself more room to slow and stop the yacht. Use a mainsail-only approach if the wind is blowing off the quay, when both wind and tide are running parallel to the quay or if a fresh wind is blowing in the opposite direction to the tide.

Headsail-only approaches can be attempted when there is an onshore wind or a fast tide running against a gentle wind.

Control of speed is everything in such manoeuvres. Make sure the mainsail can be eased right out if necessary or the jib half lowered or even dropped completely if you need to burn off speed.

When leaving, choose to depart into whichever is the strongest of the wind or tide. This will help lift the yacht clear of the jetty. If you are pinned against it, by an onshore wind for example, see if you can take a warp or anchor upwind so that you can winch the yacht gently off.

ABOVE *Warping the yacht round (see page 55). 1 Rig two new warps: one from the bow around the outside, across the stern and to the shore, the other around the stern, inside the yacht to the shore. 2 All other warps are released. Let the wind or tide push the yacht around. Fendering must be effective. 3 Rig the mooring lines as normal when alongside again.*
ABOVE LEFT *Moored alongside; note the stern line, bow line and springs.*

WARPING THE YACHT ROUND

There may be occasions when you wish to turn the yacht round, perhaps so that you can depart in a more favourable direction, or you might be moored at the head of an enclosed basin and not have enough room to turn once underway. The choice of whether to pivot around on the bow or stern will, as ever, depend on the wind or tide. You will find it difficult to swing against whichever is the strongest. But using these natural forces can make for an elegant and easy solution.

You will need extra fenders around which the yacht will turn. Then, if you are to pivot on the stern and swing the bow around, rig a new warp from the outside of the bow to lead aft around the stern, and back to the quay. Likewise rig a warp on the outside of the stern quarter, around the transom and forward inside the yacht and quay. Release all other warps and use these two to turn the yacht around.

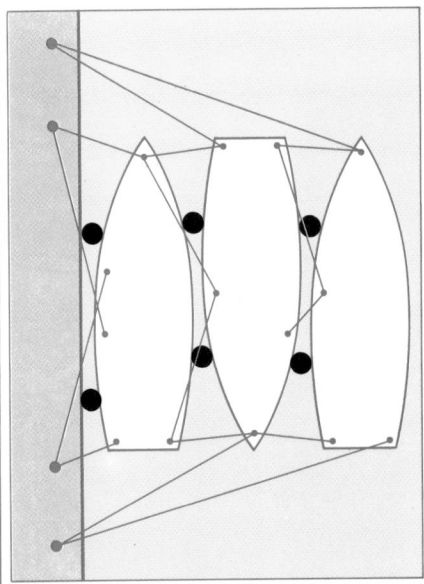

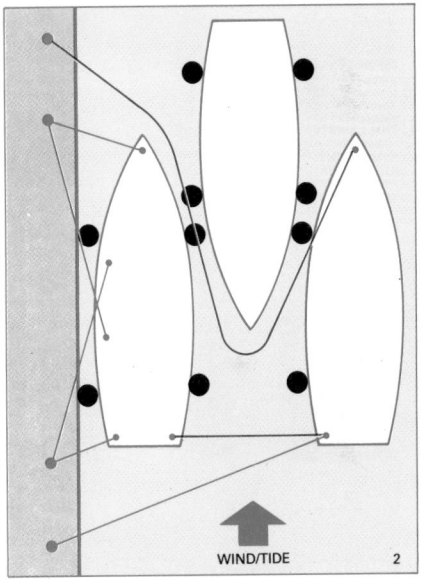

WIND/TIDE   2

RAFTING UP

If you are sailing in company, or visiting a popular harbour, it is most likely you will have to raft up with other yachts.

Be sure to ask permission of the vessel you wish to go alongside and arrange your fenders at a suitable height. You will need the usual complement of bow, stern and spring warps. In addition you will need warps long enough to run from your bow and stern to the shore, otherwise the raft will move around too much. An alternative to this is to lay anchors off your bow and stern, if the harbour master permits this practice.

Because of the shape of yachts, it can help to lie in the opposite direction to your neighbour. This will help the yachts mesh together better, keep their masts apart and allow some privacy in the cockpit.

Ask when other yachts in the raft wish to leave, as extricating one yacht from the middle is not easy. If necessary the yacht outside the departing vessel may have to let go her bow line, pass it behind, and outside, of her inside neighbour and secure it to the shore. As the departing vessel slips out, the outside vessel pulls in on her shore line to close the gap, before making fast in the normal way to her new inside neighbour.

OPPOSITE ABOVE *When a second yacht approaches a pile mooring, one method is to make fast to the existing yacht. A bow line can then be taken forward by a tender.*
OPPOSITE BELOW *Rafting up in a crowded marina.*
ABOVE LEFT *Getting ready to moor stern-to. The dinghy must be on a shortened painter.*
ABOVE *Rafting up. 1 Yachts should have bow, stern and spring warps as normal. 2 When leaving a raft slip out gently downwind/downtide; pass the bow or stern line of the outside yacht around your bow so that her crew can close up the raft.*

BOOM-ENDS

Detail of the forward end of the boom. Note the reef pendants emerging through the gooseneck. The lever is used to jam them off.

Detail of the after end of the boom. Note the clew outhaul used to tension the foot of the sail. The reef pendants go up to the leech of the mainsail.

HANDLING UNDER SAIL

Getting the best out of one's yacht under sail is a great satisfaction. Fortunately there are always improvements to be made to technique and equipment, and no manoeuvre is ever quite the same twice. Because there is always something new to learn the sailing bug can last a lifetime.

SETTING SAIL

On the conventional Bermudan rig there are two principal sails, the headsail or jib forward of the mast and the mainsail abaft of it. Both are triangular and the corners and edges bear the same names.

Dinghy sailors will be familiar with the terms although they will find the gear to control the sails more complex. Taking the corners first, the bottom corner at the front is called the tack while that at the back end of the sail is the clew. At the top is the head. In between the tack and the head is the front or leading edge of the sail known as the luff, the trailing edge between head and clew is the leech while the bottom between clew and tack is simply called the foot.

The mainsail and headsail differ in the way they are set. The headsail's or jib's luff is set on the forestay while the mainsail is attached to the mast. The jib's foot is free, while that of the mainsail is attached to the boom. For this reason, there is far greater control over the mainsail than any other sail.

THE MAINSAIL

Hoisting the mainsail is quite straightforward. First, find the foot, from it locate the clew and feed it into the gooseneck end of the boom. When the foot is stretched out straight, shackle the tack cringle or eye onto the fitting by the gooseneck and tension the outhaul attached from another eye at the clew to the end of the boom. A small purchase may be fitted for this, or merely a lanyard which is looped through and through.

Returning to the front end of the boom, work along the luff of the mainsail from the tack upwards. This will remove any twists in it. At the head there will be another cringle or more heavily reinforced headboard to which the halyard is attached. Again look out for twists — the halyard may be caught around the shrouds or a spreader end. Then feed the head into the groove on the aft face of the mast. There should be some sort of feeder here – either just a soft-mouthed opening, or if slides are attached to the luff, a 'gate' arrangement.

Before hoisting the mainsail, make sure the battens are in the leech. These help support the mainsail's trailing edge. If they are tapered, ensure the thinner end goes into the belly of the sail and if the battens are of different length, mark which pocket they belong to. Generally, the two small ones go top and bottom with the larger pair in between. A sensible precaution is to lightly stitch over the end of the pocket, to keep the battens from shaking out accidentally.

With the mainsheet (which controls the mainsail) eased, the sail is ready for hoisting. Make sure that the yacht is head to wind and that all the sail ties are off. The luff should be tensioned so that it is firm but not stretched. If a topping lift is rigged to the after end of the boom, this can be released after hoisting.

The halyard can be cleated-off and the halyard coiled. Some modern yachts now have a rope clutch or jammer for their halyard. If a conventional horn cleat is used, the halyard should be taken around once, then in a figure-of-eight, and either jammed off with another complete loop or a locking hitch. Some yachtsmen disapprove of the latter practice, but if it is done carefully, synthetic halyards can be released under load. Coil the halyard with a twist in each loop to flatten the rope. When there's about 3ft (1m) of rope left, take three turns around the coil and pull the last one through from the back, over the top of the coil and hook it onto the top horn of the cleat.

HOISTING THE MAINSAIL

The mainsail is ready for hoisting. The sail is held in the luff groove of the mast by slides.

The yacht should be head to wind when the mainsail is hoisted. Take care not to overtension the sail.

THE HEADSAIL

Much the same applies to the headsail. If the sail has been bagged correctly, the tack will be the first corner to come out of the bag. This is attached either to a special stemhead fitting or with a shackle which is kept captive on the sail or on the fitting itself.

Then the luff must be attached to the forestay. Metal snap shackles or piston hanks are used and, as with the mainsail, work up from the tack to remove twists. Once the sail is secure, the bag can be unclipped from the lifelines and taken below.

Returning to the foredeck, you can collect the halyard from the mast and after looking aloft to make sure it is not fouled, attach it to the head. Finally, the sheets need to be attached, one per side with neat bowlines. Such knots are preferable to shackles, in case a flogging sail accidentally hits the crew. If the sail is not to be hoisted straightaway, secure it to the guardrails with sail ties.

SAIL TRIM

Trimming and turning the rig for maximum efficiency is important both to the cruising passage maker and the racing crew. The latter may be trimming their sails to two decimal places on the speedo. Most crews don't bother to go to such extremes. But remember that a quarter of a knot speed improvement will mean that an 'extra' mile is gained every four hours.

A means of monitoring the sails is fundamental to good trim, so a good number of telltales is necessary on the mainsail and jibs. Telltales are small tufts of wool (or lengths of magnetic recording tape which do not stick to sails) which stream in the air flow. They should be attached to both sides of jibs, about four of them evenly spaced just in from the luff.

On the mainsail, telltales should be attached to the leech by the batten pockets. This is because both sails work in unison as an aerodynamic surface. The golden rule is to trim the front of the jib and the back of the mainsail.

BELOW *The mainsail is dropped and replaced by the smaller, more rugged storm trysail.*

THE SHEET TRACK

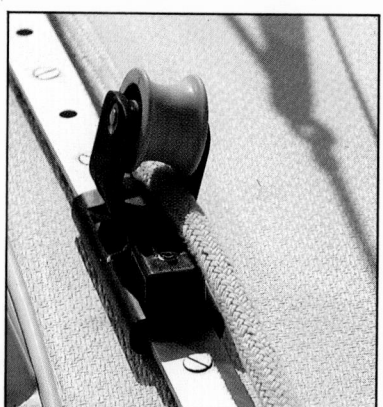

The sheet track aligns the jib sheet between the clew of the sail and the winch.

ABOVE *Halyards coiled on the mast.*
OPPOSITE ABOVE *A well-designed cockpit area gives you maximum control and allows you to enjoy the best of the elements.*
OPPOSITE BELOW *The headsail made ready to hoist.*

UPWIND

In light air, we do not need much halyard tension, just enough to take the creases out of the luff. As the wind increases, tighten the main and jib halyards to flatten the sail.

Before you trim the jib, set the lead to apply equal sheet load to foot and leech. If the foot is tight and the leech loose, then the lead is too far aft and vice versa.

If telltales are fitted, the aim is to have them streaming uniformly. If those at the bottom flutter while those at the top stream, then the lead is too far aft again, and vice versa.

When the telltales react in unison, trim can be checked. If they stream evenly on both sides of the sail then a good attached air flow has been achieved. If only the windward telltales flutter then the sheet is too slack, the helmsman is steering too high, or both. When the leeward telltales lift or flutter, the reverse applies: the sail is oversheeted or the boat is being steered too low.

Achieving nice streaming of the leech telltales on the mainsail is difficult. The really tricky part is making the top one stream because the wind speed is faster at the top of the sail than lower down. Hence you need to twist the sail. Try easing the mainsheet and hauling the traveller up the track, a little to windward.

In heavier winds, apply more sheet tension and move the traveller down to reduce effort on the helm.

Upwind efficiency is difficult to achieve. Work hard at it because you are not only beating into the wind, but usually the waves as well.

FETCHING

This is a slightly freer course than close-hauled. Yachts which are not good performers often sail better upwind fetching, rather than beating. If the seas are stopping the yacht excessively, cracking off can boost progress.

CLOSE REACHING

Halfway between a beat and a beam reach, this is a good course for covering the miles. The sheets are eased, the rig produces good forward drive and the yacht crosses the wave pattern at an easier angle.

Yachts in the 25 to 40ft (8 to 12m) range sail well on a close reach in coastal waters, because they fit neatly into the waves generated by winds up to Force 6 (25 knots), travelling diagonally across the wave pattern.

BEAM REACH

With the wind at right angles to the yacht and its apparent speed reduced, the sail controls can be eased. So, out with the sheets and down with the halyards to make the sails rounder in section. The mainsheet traveller should be down the track as well.

BROAD REACH

More easing of sheets and halyards is needed as you come on to a broad reach. Here the yacht should make her best speed for a given set of conditions. The course should not only be fast but dry as well, because the yacht is travelling with the wave pattern.

The sails can be made even fuller by easing the clew outhaul on the mainsail and moving the jib lead forward. This will also help set the jib away from the blanketing effect of the mainsail.

Some kicking strap, or vang, tension will be needed on the mainsail to stop the boom rising but not so much as to make the leech very tight.

ABOVE *An example of high-performance sail trim: running goosewinged downwind with a poled-out jib.*
RIGHT *Travelling upwind close-hauled with two headsails set.*
OPPOSITE *The spinnaker increases sail area for downwind sailing.*

RUNNING

One of the paradoxes of sailing is that running directly away from the wind is not necessarily the fastest course. This is because the yacht's own progress reduces the speed of wind acting on the rig. There is also less lift being generated as good flow off the sails is difficult to achieve.

All the rig controls will be well eased. The jib might need to be brought around and 'goosewinged' to weather to free it from the shelter of the mainsail. To keep it there will require accurate steering. In fresh conditions, a gybe preventer can be fitted to the boom to hold it forward and down.

ABOVE *While the helmsman holds a course fairly close-hauled, the crew prepares to make fine adjustments to the headsail sheet, using the winch.*

WINCHES

If progressing from a dinghy, winches will be new and important items of equipment the crew will have to learn to use properly.

By using different sized cogs, a winch can make life much easier for handling large loads. If a winch handle is turned through 360° and the drum revolves once, the winch operates as 1:1. To make life easier, winches offer 3:1, 6:1, 16:1 and even 32:1 where loads are very heavy.

The winch drum diameter and handle length vary. On the average cruiser racer, you can expect to find two-speed winches. When tensioning a halyard or headsail sheet for instance, you will find that you can start winding in one direction to obtain a 3:1 advantage. As the load increases, wind the winch in the opposite direction to obtain a 16:1 advantage.

To use a winch, the rope has to be loaded onto it correctly. Although the handle may turn in either direction, the winch drum always revolves in a clockwise direction. Take the slack out of the halyard or sheet and then place three turns onto the winch drum. If you are in any doubt as to which way the winch revolves, spin the drum first. Try and work with your fingers away from the winch drum as trapping them can be painful.

Insert the handle into the top, using your free hand to locate it into the socket properly. Then brace yourself securely and wind. Either hold the rope tail in your spare hand or, better still, pass it to another crew member.

When easing a sheet or halyard do not underestimate the load it may be under. Use the friction between the rope and the drum to control the surge. Do this by holding the flat of your hand around the drum while the other hand surges the tail. To release the rope from the drum completely do not unwind it. A better and quicker method is to pull the tail sharply upwards from the drum.

Riding turns are the winch user's number one enemy. They occur where the turns on the drum cross and lock solid; this is caused either by the rope not leading correctly into the winch drum, or by careless loading.

Sometimes riding turns can be wound out. A safer method is to take the load off the riding turn. This can be done by using a second warp attached to the first by a rolling hitch and then tensioned on another winch. When all the strain is taken up, free the fouled sheet, reload the winch and ease the load from the relieving sheet back to the original.

One variation on the standard style of winch is the self-tailer. This has a grooved channel around the top of the winch which grips the rope automatically as it is wound in. Self-tailers are a great boon but they cost more.

TACKING

Tacking a yacht is the same as tacking a dinghy, but winches take some of the effort out of handling the much larger sails, while the skipper must coordinate the crew.

To prepare for a tack, the skipper should check the area to weather of the yacht. The crew pull in the slack on the new jib sheet and load it onto the winch. The call of 'Ready About' warns the crew on deck, and also anyone below working in the galley or at the chart table.

When the crew is ready, the helmsman calls 'Lee Ho' and steers the boat through the wind. The crew releases the old sheet, checks for kinks which might jam in the headsail lead block, and pulls in on the new side.

The helmsman can slow the turn down once the yacht has gone through the wind to make it easier for the crew to wind on the winches. He might also luff a little, once the yacht is established on the new tack, to allow the crew to sheet home the last couple of inches.

If there is a large crew, one of them can guide the sail around the mast and lift its skirt over the guardrails as it is sheeted in.

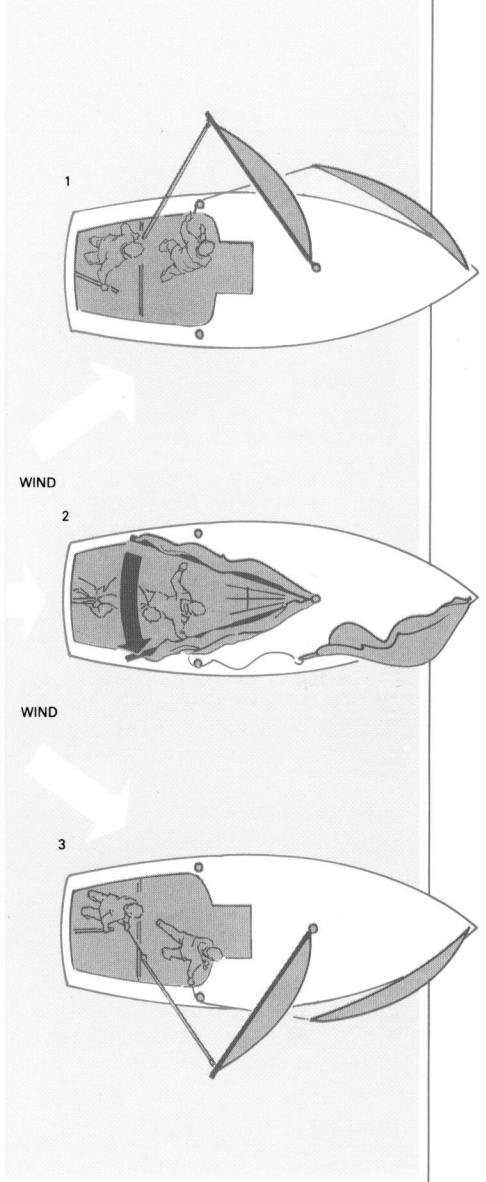

GYBING

Whereas tacking or going about sees the *bow* pass through the wind, gybing requires the *stern* to pass through. Tacking is more straightforward, for both jib and mainsail turn about their captive leading edges (on the forestay and mast) and the wind is spilled from them during the manoeuvre.

In a gybe this does not happen. The sails stay full the whole time and if they are not sheeted in beforehand in preparation, they will sweep unchecked through a large arc from one side of the boat to the other.

Controlling the sweep of the boom, in particular, is important as accidental gybes can both injure crew members and damage rig.

To gybe, the skipper checks the water he will be sailing into and warns the crew: 'Ready to gybe'. The crew take up the slack on the headsail sheet not in use. The skipper progressively sheets in the mainsail until it is almost over the centreline. He makes sure the traveller is jammed and with a call of 'Gybe Ho' he gybes the boat, slowing the turn as the boom changes sides.

The crew meanwhile will have pulled in the new sheet before releasing the old sheet to stop the jib wrapping itself around the forestay.

ABOVE LEFT *An example of goosewinging the sail in order to allow it free air.*
ABOVE *The correct procedure for a safe gybe. 1 The crew tends the jib while the helmsman hauls the mainsheet until the boom is central. 2 The stern is steered through the eye of the wind and the boom passes overhead. 3 The jib and mainsail are trimmed on the new tack.*

REEFING

The controls you will need to work will be the main halyard, the topping lift (if fitted), the mainsheet, the vang or kicking strap and the reef pendant.

How the crew is deployed depends on whether the main halyard and reef pendant are both mounted aft by the cockpit, both mounted on or near the

mast or split between the two. If there is a big enough crew one person can be allocated to halyard and one to reef pendant. If there is just

one crew member available, the same sequence is followed, with one task completed before the next stage is tackled.

REEFING

The method of reefing the mainsail varies from system to system. Older vessels will probably have roller reefing where the sail is progressively rolled up around the boom. Modern yachts will have the near universal slab reefing system whereby fixed amounts of sail are pulled down.

With both systems it is vital to have the sails empty of wind when reefing. There is no point in straining against a sail still trying to drive the yacht.

1. Ease the mainsheet and kicking strap to spill wind from the sail.

2. Tension the topping lift.

3. Release the main halyard and pull luff down the mast until the reef cringle can be hooked on to the claw at the gooseneck.

4. Tension the main halyard. If the breeze is fresh, you will want a lot of tension to flatten the sail.

5. Pull down on the reef pendant. Normally this emerges from the boom at the gooseneck and will shorten the leech the same amount as you have just reduced the luff. If the sail is shaking with no wind in it, there should be little load on the pendant. If there is, check to see if the kicking strap and mainsheet are still loose. Pull the last inch or so of the pendant home, using a winch if one is available and jam off the pendant.

REEFING: JIB CHANGE

The reefed mainsail is set again.

The next reduction of sail area is a smaller jib.

6. Release the topping lift. Now sheet in. The sail can be tidied up. If you have a long upwind beat ahead of you, put a sail tie around the boom and through the reef cringle in case the pendant breaks. If you have tied up the loose belly of the sail, this simple precaution could save it from considerable damage.

Remember if conditions are such that a reef is needed, the crew should be wearing their safety harnesses!

A properly slab-reefed mainsail can be very efficient. Good pendant and halyard tension is essential to flatten the sail. There's little point in making the sail smaller if it has a large belly still making the yacht heel over.

For roller reefing the drill is much the same:
1. Release the halyard and kicking strap.
2. Take up on the topping lift.
3. Roll the sail down.
4. Release the topping lift and re-tension the halyard.

Getting a good set with a rolled mainsail takes more practice than slab reefing. Because the leech is longer than the luff and because the luff is held firm by the mast as it is rolled onto the boom, it is difficult to achieve equal tension all along the boom. Consequently, the sail is often bellied because the leech has not been pulled out sufficiently, and the boom end droops. In rough conditions, the low boom sweeping the cockpit is best avoided. One answer is to roll a sail bag into the leech to reduce the drop. The kicking strap will need a claw to fit around the rolled sail on the boom.

CHANGING HEADSAILS

Sail area can also be reduced by changing headsails. The order in which you reduce the sail plan varies from boat to boat. With a masthead rigged yacht, the headsails are both larger and more numerous, so you can expect to change headsails more often than would be the case with a fractional rigger. Sail will be reduced in roughly equal amounts between mainsail and headsails, with the jib being the first step in each reduction. With a fractional rig, the first change will be to a small jib and thereafter only the mainsail need be reefed successively, unless conditions are especially severe.

Headsail changing can be made easier if the sail bags are marked clearly as to which sail they contain, if each corner of every sail is marked 'Head', 'Tack' and 'Clew' as appropriate and if the helmsman bears away for the duration of the change to make the foredeck a drier and steadier place to work.

First, the existing headsail has to be dropped. Ease both the sheet and the halyard. If shorthanded the person on the foredeck can take the halyard forward and lower it himself as the sail is pulled down. The helmsman can also luff up so that the sail drops inside the guardrails and not over the side. The halyard can be unclipped from the head of the jib and attached to the pulpit. Then undo the sheets, free the tack and bag the sail. Make sure the tack is the last corner to vanish into the bag and, if possible, pass the drawstring of the sail bag through the tack cringle to keep it ready for the next time it is used.

Bring the new sail forward along the weather deck from the companionway, unless it is calm enough to use the forehatch. Tie the bag to the guardrails and hoist as normal. Once the sheet is attached, remember to move the lead position ready for the new sail.

You can speed up the change by bending on the new sail to the forestay, while the original sail is still set. You can do this if there is sufficient space between the tack and first hank of the original sail for the hanks of the replacement to fit in.

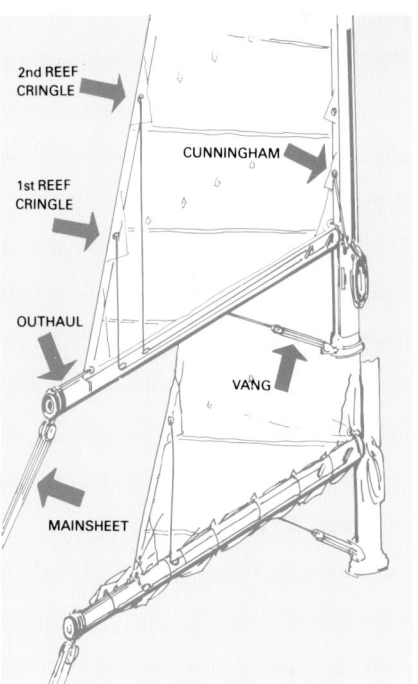

2nd REEF CRINGLE

CUNNINGHAM

1st REEF CRINGLE

OUTHAUL

VANG

MAINSHEET

OPPOSITE *A heavily reefed mainsail, and a small jib set.*
TOP *Reefed-down in squally conditions.*
LEFT *Changing the headsail.*
ABOVE *Mainsail controls.*

ABOVE *A roller-furled headsail.*
ABOVE RIGHT *The outhaul and halyard are tensioned to give the mainsail an effective aerofoil shape.*

REEFING JIBS

Some owners have headsails which can be reefed, the idea being that they avoid the expense of buying a smaller sail. Like the slab-reefing mainsail there is an extra cringle on both the luff and the leech with a row of reef points in between.

There are two main ways to reef such a jib. The first entails dropping it, but the second can be done underway.

The simplest way is to drop it, attach the upper luff cringle to the tack fitting on the stem head, move the sheet up the leech, tie in the reef points, and after moving the lead position on the track, re-hoist. .

If you do it underway, you will need a spare jib sheet or the use of the weather jib sheet. Attach the new sheet to the upper cringle on the leech and either bring it aft to a second lead block on the headsail track, or pass it through the lead block in use if the block will accept two sheets at once.

Then rig another line from the stemhead, up the luff of the jib, through the cringle and back aft to a cleat via a block on the bow. The idea is that when the halyard is eased, you can pull on this line and bring the new luff cringle down to the tack fitting.

As before, it is important to tie the reef in, in case a wave fills the bunt of the sail and damages it.

ROLLER HEADSAILS

Roller headsails are becoming increasingly popular both on large yachts and small charter boats. The gear is becoming lighter, more reliable and sailmakers are cutting sails better than ever to match the characteristics of the gear.

Such sails generally have high clews and appear more like an equilateral triangle in shape to ensure they roll up evenly. They also tend to be cut flatter than normal sails for the same reason.

Roller furling jibs are a popular item on the options list of most boatbuilders; a competent handyman can retro-fit such gear.

What are the disadvantages? Firstly, sail shape is compromised. When they are furled in stronger winds they don't give the same efficient foil as a smaller, heavy air jib so that the yacht's pointing can suffer by some 5–15°. And in really heavy weather, a storm jib will still have to be set. This will entail the need either for a second stay inside the furling gear or the removal of the roller headsail from

LEFT *A roller-furling headsail. Any ordinary jib or genoa can be used on the roller furling system.*
ABOVE *The headsail roller-furling gear.*

ABOVE *The pole is held in position by lift and the downhaul.*

its luff foil and the setting of the storm jib in its place. This will mean changing the biggest headsail for the smallest in conditions that can only be difficult. For most people, however, these sails are ideal for most of the time.

Roller jibs are controlled just like a normal jib except that on one side of the yacht a control line will run aft from the drum at the bottom of the luff foil to a cleat or winch in the cockpit. To unfurl the jib, un-cleat the control line and winch in on the jib sheet. Don't let go of the control line. If the furling drum spins too fast, the control line can jam inside it.

To furl the jib, ease the jib sheet and pull in on the control line. If the line is heavily loaded, ease the sheet more. Rolling in against some jib sheet tension ensures a tight furl. You will need to adjust the lead position on the track each time the jib is rolled in or out.

Most furling jibs come with a coloured band on their leeches to protect the sail cloth when they are left rolled up. It is a wise precaution to secure such jibs with a sail tie. Better still hoist a sausage-like sail cover over them for maximum protection from wind and ultra-violet light.

STORM SAILS

Not only do a storm jib and a trysail reduce the amount of sail set, but, if they are cut correctly and trimmed properly, they can also provide enough power to drive to windward and out of danger.

Storm sails should not be treated as a last resort. Not only can they improve the yacht's speed in heavy going, but they keep the yacht more upright and hence more comfortable. They must be set before conditions have deteriorated to their worst and the crew is at its weakest.

When buying storm sails, costs can be kept reasonable if existing deck gear can be used: spinnaker blocks on the quarter for sheeting the trysail; and either the forward end of the headsail track or snatch blocks on the gunwhale for sheeting the storm jib. Savings here can be ploughed back into a nicely shaped sail, with triple stitching, reinforced corners and taping along every edge. Other points to look for are metal luff slides, not plastic ones, if the trysail sets in a groove on the mast; doubled slides or hanks at the head and tack of both sails; and wire strops to lift the sail off the deck and clear of waves.

Additionally, if you have a wire-to-rope halyard, a wire strop on the head of both sails will extend the halyard so that the wire comes all the way back to the winch drum, thus eliminating a weak link.

The storm jib is set in the normal way while there are various permutations for the trysail. It can be set either on its own private track besides the main luff groove, or, with the mainsail stowed below the luff gate, it can be hoisted in the normal track. Moreover, it can be sheeted either to the end of the boom, or directly down to the quarter.

In most circumstances it is best not to use the boom. Lash it down to the cabin top with the mainsail securely bound up.

The trysail can be stopped by tying very light lines around the leech and through the luff cringles. This keeps it under control until it is sheeted in and the lines break to open up the sail.

Two sheets are required for the trysail and both can be used to give the sail a good foil shape. Modern fin-and-skeg yachts need forward movement because their relatively small keels generate lift from the water flowing over them, rather than relying on sheer physical area to reduce leeway.

When attaching the halyard to either sail, make sure there is a large shackle available in case the normal halyard snap shackle does not fit. As soon as the jib or mainsail halyard is lowered, tie it off to the mast or pulpit, so that it is not jerked out of your hand.

Finally, make sure your storm sails are high visibility orange in colour and carry some means of identification, such as your sail number.

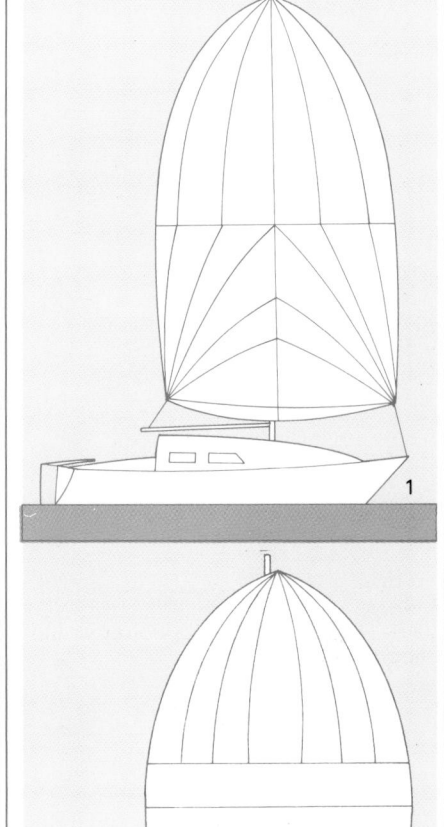

ABOVE LEFT *On a fairly calm day, the balloon-like shape of the spinnakers makes the most of the available wind.*

LEFT *On the smaller yacht, the spinnaker can be controlled with just one sheet on each side; larger yachts employ an extra lazy sheet and lazy guy when gybing.*

ABOVE *Types of spinnaker. 1 The Starcut. 2 The versatile tri-radial spinnaker.*

SPINNAKER HANDLING

Spinnakers boost downwind speed more than any other sails. Although they require more equipment and skill than other sails, the rewards are greater. There is no reason for the beginner not to have a go if they remember one simple fact: problems with spinnakers can be sorted out if the wind is removed from them. Therefore they should be hoisted and recovered in the shelter of other sails, usually the mainsail.

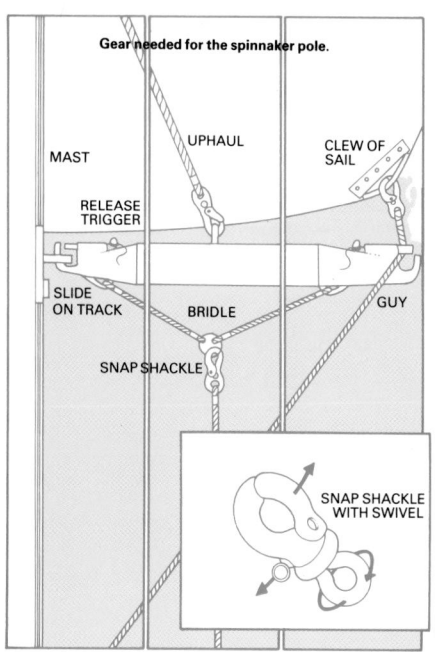

Gear needed for the spinnaker pole.

MAST

UPHAUL

CLEW OF SAIL

RELEASE TRIGGER

SLIDE ON TRACK

BRIDLE

GUY

SNAP SHACKLE

SNAP SHACKLE WITH SWIVEL

DOWNWIND SAILS

Unlike the old gaffers with their big high-peaked mainsails, the modern Bermudan sloop is underpowered downwind. There are alternatives to the spinnaker, if required.

The simplest is to use a pole to expose the headsail. It is best not to clip the pole to the clew cringle but just onto the sheet itself. Then the pole can be attached to the mast. In light airs you will want to lift the pole and in stronger conditions, proper control of the pole is essential. For this you will need an uphaul (a spare halyard or a proper pole uphaul), and a downhaul which can run from the pole end via a block on the bow and aft to the cockpit. The safest way to use the pole is to set it up to windward when the jib is still sheeted to leeward. Attach another long sheet to the jib, lead it through the pole end and aft to the quarter outside the rigging and lifelines and forward again to the cockpit. Then, when you are ready to goosewing, ease the old sheet on the jib and pull the new long sheet so that the jib clew goes to the pole end. You can reverse the process, the idea being to set and recover the pole without the jib exerting load on it.

Cruising chutes do away with the pole altogether. Cut from spinnaker cloth, these asymmetric sails are at their best reaching; without a pole they tend to collapse when running. The tack is attached to the bow and the halyard should be tightened more for reaching than for running. Cruising chutes sheet to the quarter like a spinnaker and if you attach two sheets, lead either side of the forestay, they can be gybed. This may be helpful when dropping them. It will be much easier if the chute can be brought behind the mainsail and the wind taken out of them.

Traditionalists swear by using two headsails. You don't necessarily need two forestays or a double grooved luff foil to use them. The second jib can be set flying (with just its tack attached and the halyard tightened) or on the same forestay as the first jib by alternating the hanks. Ocean passage makers use the double headed rig so that they can drop the mainsail altogether and stop it chafing against the shrouds.

SPINNAKERS

What extra gear is needed for the spinnaker? Apart from a pole, the other major hardware items are an extra pair of winches. You can use the genoa winches although the extra pair usually enable the spinnaker to be set and dropped while the headsail is still drawing.

The remaining gear is running rigging. A special halyard is desirable as it will oscillate and chafe in a normal sheave. The pole will need an uphaul and downhaul, controlled if possible from the cockpit. Finally sheets and guys are required; lead outside everything to blocks on the quarter and thence to winches in the cockpit.

Small yachts, up to 28ft (8.5m), can use just one sheet per side; the one running through the pole end is called the guy. Some means of hauling this guy down to a block amidships is needed to help stabilise the pole. On larger yachts two sheets and two guys are fitted; the sheets lead aft and the guys lead through the amidships block on the sidedeck, although only one sheet and one guy are used in combination at once. The spares, the lazy sheet and lazy guy, are used in a gybe when the sail is set on the other side.

The spinnaker must be packed correctly to avoid twists. This is achieved by running around all three sides, working outwards from the head. The head and clews are then held while the bulk of the sail is packed into the bag with the three corners left poking out ready for the halyard, sheet and guy.

The bag can be tied down near the companionway or on the sidedeck behind the jib. It is essential that the sheet on the leeward side and the guy on the windward side are led outside everything before they are clipped onto the

spinnaker clews. The pole is then set with the guy running through its outer end and the uphaul and downhaul attached.

To hoist, the halyard is pulled smartly up and made fast. During the hoist, the guy should be pulled back to bring the spinnaker clew to the pole end. The sheet should be slack during the hoist and once the sail is hoisted and halyard cleated, be brought in slowly to stop the luff (nearest the pole) from folding.

There are three prime considerations in trimming:

1. The pole should be raised or lowered to keep both clews level.

2. The pole should be eased forward or brought aft with the guy so that it is at right angles to the wind. If you bear away, draw the pole aft. If you reach up, ease the pole forward.

3. The sheet should be eased until the luff just curls and then trimmed in slightly. It should be played on this 'edge' of collapse constantly.

Gybing the spinnaker is the trickiest part for most crews. Unlike hoisting and dropping, keeping the spinnaker full during the gybe is the secret of success so that the sheet and guy are nice and taut, not flogging away and impossible to catch hold of. In a small yacht the pole is 'end-for-ended': unclip the pole off the mast; clip the pole onto the existing sheet which will become the new guy; now the pole is attached to both sheet and guy; take the pole off the old guy and transfer it to the mast. The helmsman can then gybe the boat and bring the mainsail across. Some slack on the pole lift and downhaul will be needed.

With twin sheets and guys, a 'dip-pole' gybe is used whereby the pole is lowered so that it can swing inside the forestay and out to the other side. Twin sheets and guys are needed to control the spinnaker at all times because the loads will be higher in a larger yacht. As before, keeping the sail drawing will turn a complex job into a simple one.

Make sure the pole is high enough at the mast end to clear the forestay; trip the pole off the existing guy and, by releasing the uphaul, lower it as it swings into the bow; clip the lazy guy from the other side into the pole end; raise the pole on its uphaul. The sail is now flying on its old guy (which no longer has the pole on it) and the old sheet. The aim is to transfer the load of the sail onto the new (lazy) guy and new (lazy) sheet by simultaneously easing the old guy and hauling in the new one: likewise with the sheet. As the process is nearly complete the helmsman can gybe the mainsail. The more hands available the better!

To drop the spinnaker, hoist the jib so that the spinnaker can be dropped in its shelter. The object of the drop is to ease the load off two corners so that the sail spills wind and can be gathered in easily. First either trip the clew attached to the guy by easing the pole forward to the forestay and releasing the snap shackle or, if the guy is long enough, by allowing the guy to run forward. Now the spinnaker should be just flying from the sheet and halyard, like a flag out behind the mainsail. With no wind in it, gather it in as the halyard is released.

TOP LEFT *On a beat, the sheets are trimmed in hard and the mainsheet traveller is centralized.*
TOP RIGHT *Trimming the spinnaker.*
ABOVE *A poled-out headsail set.*

CHAPTER SEVEN

ANCHORS AND ANCHORING

Anchoring is another form of mooring, where instead of picking up a fixed ground chain the yacht uses her own equipment to lay a mooring. This can be in a busy harbour, quiet roadstead or perhaps a deserted bay where the scenery allows you to enjoy one of the great satisfactions of sailing.

Above all, anchoring is fundamental to a yacht's safety. It can provide an opportunity to deal with a problem, such as engine failure, or it can enable you to wait for adverse tidal or weather conditions to change to your advantage.

EQUIPMENT

Successful anchoring is the result of having the right equipment and using it correctly. First, the yacht herself should be properly equipped. This means having a stout bow roller which is firmly attached. There should be good-sized cheeks to keep the rope or chain on the roller and these cheeks must be smooth, or have a fair lead, to prevent chafe. Above all a keep pin must be fitted to ensure that if the yacht is plunging up and down in rough water, the anchor cable does not jump clear of the roller. Yachts have been damaged, and lost, by cables coming clear of the roller and allowing the craft to swing broadside to the waves or strong tidal stream.

Today's cruiser racers are generally fitted with good bow rollers. Indeed, some have two; a smooth one for rope and a second, notched roller for chain. Some Scandinavian yachts make do with just a fairlead because they anchor rarely and when they do it is in flat water.

The anchor cable can be of rope or chain. Chain is heavier and much more expensive but is preferable. This is because its own weight helps lower the pull on the anchor as well as acting as a damper as the yacht surges against the anchor. Chain also self-stows, in that it hardly ever tangles as it is fed into its locker.

Rope however is cheaper. It also suits the modern style of yacht which has fitted-out forecabins with berths rather than the old style fo'c's'le which was used just for stowage, not as a sleeping cabin. Nowadays, foredeck lockers are often used to stow the anchor. Warp is also used because the modern fine-bowed yacht does not like weight in the bow. It is detrimental to performance.

Whether you choose rope, chain or a combination of both, be sure to mark it properly in either fathoms or metres. In the old days chain was calibrated and marked with leather thongs but today paint will suffice. On rope, whipping twine can fulfill the same function. Whichever you choose it is important to know how much you have paid out.

It is essential that the bitter-end, the end attached to the yacht, should be secured firmly to a strong part of the vessel. A small U-bolt in the bow well is not strong enough. Whether the bitter-end is attached in the well or if the chain is led belowdecks via a navel or hawse pipe, be sure to use rope and not a shackle. Rope can always be cut in an emergency, such as another yacht fouling your anchor and dragging your boat into danger, whereas a shackle cannot. If you stow your chain below deck, it helps to have this rope fastening long enough to allow the last link in the chain to emerge on deck. In this way it is easy to add a

ABOVE AND OPPOSITE *Anchoring provides an opportunity to enjoy varied and splendid scenery, which is such an important part of the pleasure of sailing.*

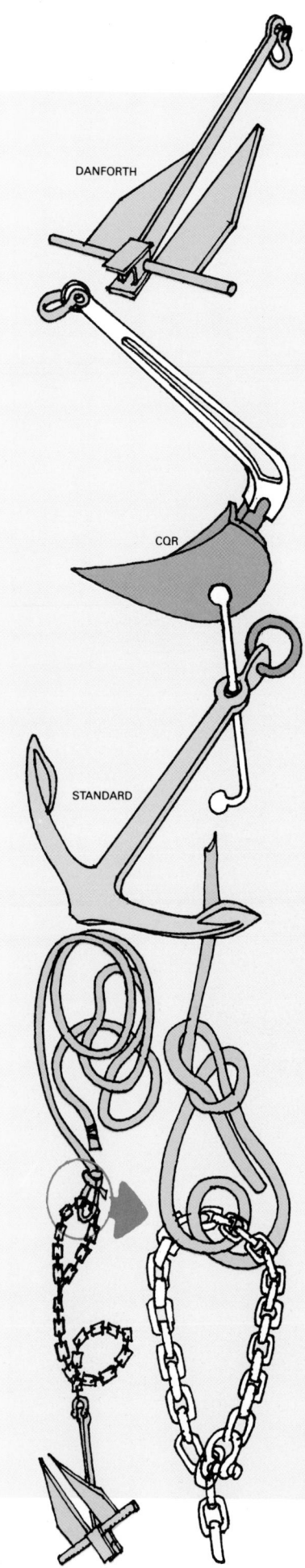

warp onto the chain should you need to lengthen the anchor cable.

Although handling the anchor is hard work it can be made easier either by stowing the anchor permanently on the bow roller, or by having a windlass, or a combination of both. If the anchor remains on the roller it must be firmly secured so that it does not come adrift and damage the yacht whilst underway. A keep pin through the shank and several stout lashings should do the job.

A windlass is a boon even for a moderate size anchor and chain, though it is of less use if rope is used. It can be manually or power operated. Often windlasses have one ribbed winch drum, or gypsy, for rope and another notched drum for chain. If they can be operated independently, so much the better.

With many boatbuilders supplying an anchor plus a chain and warp as standard you may not be faced with choosing an anchor but it is seamanlike to carry a second anchor, a kedge, and often a different type provides a choice should the main anchor fail to hold. When choosing an anchor for your boat you will need to match the yacht's displacement with the anchor manufacturer's recommendations.

ANCHOR TYPES

There are many different anchors available around the world but these are the most common:

THE STOCK ANCHOR (Fisherman, Admiralty pattern etc). An old design, this is everyone's idea of how an anchor should look. It is not so common today because modern designs have the same holding power for much less weight and are easier to stow. The pronounced flukes at either end of the long arm allow the anchor to penetrate and hold in dense weed. Most common use of this pattern today is as a back up. Collapsible versions help make this anchor easier to stow flat in a locker.

THE CQR (Plough etc). The original was designed in 1933 to anchor Flying Boats and the name is a corruption of 'secure'. This type affords excellent holding on all types of bottom except thick weed. Should it drag, the clever design allows the anchor to plough itself in again. Many consider the genuine forged CQR the finest anchor available for most circumstances.

THE DANFORTH (Meon, Brittany etc). Designed in America in 1939, by one R. Danforth, there are now a number of similar designs. The idea is that the heavy crown sinks the anchor. The wide, pointed spade-like flukes hinge either side of the shank and dig in when a low pull is applied. The type offers excellent holding in sand and mud. But if it breaks free and the yacht drags it does not bite again as often as the CQR. It does stow flat, however.

THE BRUCE Newest of the yacht anchors is the Bruce, developed to keep oil rigs stationary in severe seas such as those found in the North Sea where they proved to have very high holding power for a given weight. This is an attraction for yachtsmen as it allows them to carry, and handle, a lighter anchor. The Bruce also offers good holding power on a short rode. But with no hinges and a claw-like shape, it is very awkward to stow on anything other than a roller.

OPPOSITE *An anchorage off Turkey.*

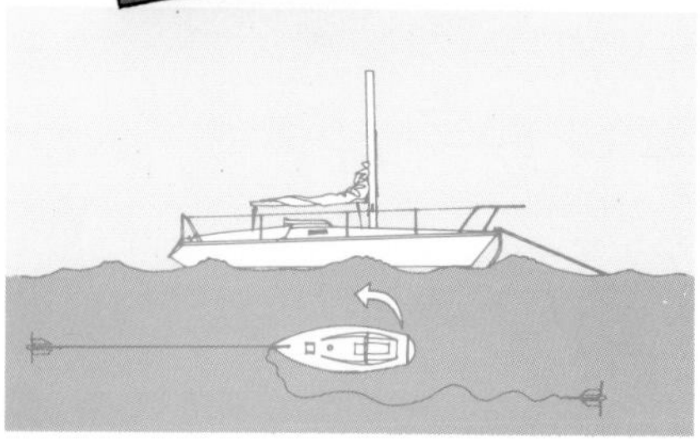

TOP *A Caribbean anchorage.*
ABOVE *Lying to two anchors. This may be necessary when a tide change will turn the yacht through 180° or where space is restricted.*
RIGHT *A well planned foredeck, with anchor, windlass, bollard, two fairleads and large cleats.*
OPPOSITE *Scottish solitude.*

What other equipment is needed? A deck scrubber is a good idea so that mud and sand from the sea bed doesn't foul the decks. A pair of gloves saves the hands. You'll need a ball-shape by day and an all-round white light at night to show you are anchored. A light line and fender or special buoy is needed if you use a tripping line. This marks the spot above your anchor and can help free it if it fouls another rode or underwater obstruction. Pulling on the tripping line attached to the crown of the anchor usually lifts the flukes clear of an obstruction.

Finally, some form of weight or 'angel' can be used if you are having trouble holding. The weight – it might be a special heavy piece of metal or just a few loops of chain – helps damp the surge on the cable, lowers the angle of pull on the anchor and reduces the yacht's swinging room.

TECHNIQUE

There are three main considerations when anchoring. First, you need to know the depth of the water, remembering to allow for the rise and fall of the tide or changes in water level due to barometric pressure changes. Secondly, you need to know the nature of the bottom. The chart will show the composition of the sea bed while greater detail can be obtained from pilots and cruising guides. Thirdly, you must assess the suitability of the anchorage in terms of traffic and safety, should conditions deteriorate.

As in many aspects of sailing, preparation goes a long way to making difficult tasks simple. Having made your assessment of where to anchor, brief the crew. Work out a simple system of hand signals so that helmsman and foredeck hand can slow the yacht down, stop, go left, right or astern and let go the anchor without shouting or confusion. This can help the family crew, where father might give the helm over to mother so that he can handle the heavy work forward.

Next, prepare the chain or rope. This can be flaked out on deck or in the well. If you are using all chain you will need three to four times the depth of water and six to seven times if you are using rope with just a little chain. In rough conditions, more still will be needed.

When picking a spot in a busy anchorage it will help to anchor in company with boats of the same size and with the same anchor cable so that the yachts lie in a similar fashion. The seamanlike sailor will assess the other yachts and choose to anchor to leeward of one with stout ground tackle laid. Certainly it is best to keep well clear of any suspect yachts which look as if they might drag.

You should aim for a reasonable gap unless you are fortunate to have the anchorage to yourself. Imagine a circle on the water whose circumference is described by the length of your yacht plus half the length of rope or chain you intend to put out. Your perfect gap would be a circle twice as big again. If you drop the anchor at the edge of the circle you can then drop back to its centre.

Unless the engine is inoperative, or you have the skill to match your confidence, anchoring is best done under power. This gives you total control and clear decks, although it is sensible to have the sail still ready for hoisting should the engine fail and leave you out of control.

Motor up to your chosen spot. With the way taken off the boat, let out (veer) the cable until the anchor lands on the seabed. Using wind, tide or reverse thrust, let the yacht drop astern as you veer more rope or chain.

When you have veered most of the set length, cleat off the cable and see if the anchor has buried. Holding the cable forward of the roller you should feel chain lift off the seabed and tug at the anchor. Because rope stretches, you can feel it go taut if the anchor is holding the yacht. Often you can feel the anchor dragging along the bottom if it has not bitten, in which case you will have to re-lay it.

It is important not to drop the anchor and chain in a heap on the seabed. *Laying* an anchor describes precisely what has to be done.

THE KEDGE

A light anchor of any type is known as a kedge. The Danforth makes a good kedge. Here the kedge is flaked, or laid out ready for use.

OTHER TECHNIQUES

Part of the magic of sailing is freedom from noise, though anchoring without using an engine is not for the inexperienced. You may want to try if under sail in a quiet anchorage, however, and if approaching up wind, do so under mainsail alone so as to keep boatspeed moderate and the foredeck clear from the headsail. Ease sheets and luff to drop the anchor. If you try it downwind, use just the jib or try bare poles if there is any sort of breeze. If all goes to plan you will drop the anchor, sail past it and as you reach the end of the scope you can round up into the wind and snub the 'hook' home.

There are occasions when two anchors, the main bower and the kedge, can be laid. The most common are if the weather turns nasty and you need more secure holding, or if you want to restrict the yacht's swinging room.

If you have laid the first anchor in the normal way, you can motor slowly forward and drop another to the left or right. When the yacht drops back, she should lie with the anchors laid out in a Vee ahead.

The second anchor may be laid from a dinghy. Row away from the bow at an approximate 45° angle having first flaked out the chain or rope in the dinghy. This should run out as you row. Try tying the anchor over the stern of the dinghy so that it can be dropped to the bottom by just slipping a knot or hitch – a much safer method than trying to throw a heavy anchor over from a small dinghy.

If the tide turns or the wind swings through 180° you might find two anchors get into a tangle. One way to avoid this is to set the first one, then pay out twice the length of cable you need before dropping the second one. Next, take up half the length of the first cable until the yacht lies at the mid-point. Then shackle the chains together, or lash the ropes, and lower them so that they are below the level of the keel. This way you have created a swivel about which the yacht can turn.

Whichever method you choose, you ought to double check that the anchor is holding fast. Stand at the bow and either take bearings of fixed objects on the shore or line them up in a transit. A change in the bearing or transit indicates the yacht is moving. Some modern electronic aids such as depth sounders and position indicators have alarms which can prove helpful. Best of all though are our natural senses. Sailors develop a feel for a sound or some such clue which indicates the yacht is dragging. If you have any doubts, stand an anchor watch or at least have a look out of the hatch a number of times during the night.

ABOVE LEFT AND BELOW LEFT *Relaxing in the Caribbean. When choosing a site, check what the holding ground is like on the appropriate chart for the area or in a pilot book, or employ the lead line.*

TOP *Approaching an Australian anchorage.*
ABOVE *The mechanical windlass makes handling the anchor and chain easier.*

CHAPTER EIGHT

FIRST CRUISE: FIRST RACE

ABOVE *The galley; the cooker is gimballed to allow for heel.*
OPPOSITE *Under sail off the coast of Yugoslavia.*

Planning the first cruise can be enjoyable in itself. Preparation of the yacht should begin early while the cruise route should be carefully planned with several built-in foul weather alternatives.

Tide and wind considerations are fundamental to the plan. It is helpful to work to windward early on in the cruise so that the return journey is, hopefully, downwind. Timing the tides will affect many aspects. Rounding headlands or making passages in wind-against-tide situations are plainly less preferable than when wind and tide are running the same way. Working with tide can cut down passage time markedly, while some harbours or anchorages can only be approached on the flood.

Where possible, approaches to the shore should be made in daylight and heaving-to offshore, or sailing reciprocal courses offshore until daylight, may be more prudent than attempting a strange harbour entrance in darkness.

Sometimes the cruise may call for at least one long passage. This is best tackled early with a fresh and strong crew. Ideally this crew should include some balance of experience, so that the skipper is not the only capable person aboard. If you plan a night sail or a passage long enough for watches to be used, an experienced mate is essential.

REPORTING

In most countries around the world, the maritime rescue services are coordinated by the coastguard. Many offer a reporting service so that a friendly eye can be kept on your progress. In Britain, for example, HM Coastguard operate the CG66 pre-paid card system. A skipper can pick up a card in his yacht club, marina, Coastguard Station or from the Harbour Master and file his passage plan. Upon arriving at each destination he can notify the Coastguard by VHF or telephone so that a track of his movements can be kept or a change of plan noted. A tear-off section can be kept by shore-side contacts, should they wish to reach the yacht.

PROVISIONING

Compared with day sails, a cruise places a much greater strain on the limited galley facilities onboard. This does not deter some cruising yachtsmen from enjoying a full roast dinner!

A day-to-day plan will assist greatly in victualling up and using food in the correct rotation so that fresh foodstuffs don't spoil. Two-pot cookery is quite common onboard as it makes efficient use of the limited number of burners. Convenience food can be turned into very presentable meals with suitable seasoning and simple garnishing.

Stock up with plenty of energy boosters such as chocolate, fruit and biscuits, while hot beverages and cool soft drinks are vital for sustenance.

The cruise plan should allow for taking on extra water, fresh food and, something never to be neglected, fuel.

The crew will expend a great deal of energy at sea, particularly in cold weather. Plenty of hot food is essential.

Rest is vital to an enjoyable passage. Note the berth's leecloth.

WATCH KEEPING

If the cruise features a 24-hour long sail, or longer, some form of watch keeping will be necessary. Even on shorter passages, the crew should be encouraged to rest, and the skipper ought to get some sleep 'in the bank' when the going is good.

As the weather worsens, so running the yacht becomes more tiring and proper rest is vital for efficient, safe handling of the vessel.

Watches can split the crew in half, on a four hours on, four hours off, basis. On longer passages a more popular system is to run two six-hour watches during the day, reverting to four-hour periods at night.

Another alternative is the more informal 'buddy' system where crew members are paired off and one rests at times agreed with the other partner.

NIGHT SAILING

A passage of more than 10 hours or so will inevitably involve sailing at night. First timers are usually nervous and may be disorientated. Once the 'fear barrier' is crossed many find sailing at night an immensely rewarding experience.

Careful preparation is needed. All possible navigation work which can be done in advance should be, ie identifying buoys, lights, shoals, transits, etc. Every system should be checked, particularly navigation lights. Anything which may be required during the night, such as the next sail in the event of a sail change, should be made accessible. If a sail change is necessary, see if it can be done at a change of watch. Make sure that anyone on deck at night is wearing a safety harness and is clipped on.

When changing watches, a hot drink is the traditional welcome from those coming off watch to those going on. Although the yacht sails just the same at night as in day, our perception of it is different. The boat seems to move faster, the wind seems fresher and our sense of distance is distorted. At the change of watch, the helmsman should talk the new person through relevant information such as surrounding shipping, the most recent forecast and tell him or her if any gear has been moved or rigged.

Waking the skipper needlessly is not a crime and he should certainly be called if anyone on deck has any uncertainty about anything. The skipper, for his part, is best advised to stand his watch in the period before dawn. The night is at its coldest then; a new wind may come in with the morning and exhaustion among the crew will be at its greatest, so he must make the best use of his experience.

FIRST RACE

Most sailors have a natural competitive edge. Even the annual cruise in company can spur the most hardened cruising skipper into battling for line honours, while for others, competitive sailing may exclude all other types.

It would be unreasonable to expect to win your first race, especially if you have not had a crack at it before in smaller boats, dinghies or perhaps as crew with another skipper. Too many places are thrown away by simple errors and if you can eliminate those in your first couple of races there is no reason why you should not finish in mid-fleet. Thereafter, progress up the fleet is tough, and only experience and practice will yield improvements.

INSURANCE

The first consideration is to check to see if your insurance covers racing risks. If not, an extra premium may be necessary; but finding cover for racing to include spar damage, without a large waiver on each claim, is becoming increasingly difficult.

LEFT *The chart table and galley in use; space is at a premium even on the larger yacht, so the crew must be tidy and organized.*

MEASUREMENT

Even if your yacht is a one-design, whereby all yachts are as similar as practicable, you will need a measurement certificate. For one-designs this will confirm that the yacht has been built to the class rule, while for other yachts the certificate will depend on having the yacht actually measured. From this data a formal handicap formula can be obtained so that a correction can be applied to the yacht's elapsed finishing time and a corrected time result obtained. This allows dissimilar yachts to compete against each other in the same race.

Measurement systems like these can be as crude as the local club handicap (worked out amid great mystery behind closed doors), or as complex as the International Offshore Rule (IOR) which rates monohulls from 18ft to 80ft (5.5 to 25m) LOA. At present it is the only international rule and due to its cost and complexity it is favoured predominantly by grand-prix yachts.

In 1985, the Offshore Racing Council (ORC), the body which administers the IOR, adopted a second tier rule which they hope will appeal to weekend club racers all over the world. This is the International Measurement System and the aim of it is to provide a low cost, but relatively sophisticated means of handicapping yachts. Not only does the yacht have to conform to measurement but her sails also.

RACE ENTRY

With insurance and certificate in order you may enter a race. Do so early, to avoid the extra cost and inconvenience of a late entry. More importantly, entering early means that you can obtain the sailing instructions. Studying them will tell you which buoys will be used to select the course from, start times, and what mandatory equipment has to be carried. One-design classes and offshore races will normally be subject to class rules or Special Regulations of the Offshore Racing Council. The organizing club may add or delete its own requirements. Make sure, therefore, you are not carrying too much or too little gear.

YACHT AND CREW

The yacht herself will have to be made ready for racing. The whole subject of tuning is immense and covered frequently in books and magazines. Don't be afraid to ask those who are doing well in your class for advice. Above all, avoid the two major mistakes which can irrecoverably slow your performance. One is

not having the mast perpendicular. A surprisingly common situation, you can check for it by taking the main halyard out to the chainplate on one side then the other and adjusting the bottlescrews on the standing rigging until the halyard falls in the same spot either side.

The second fundamental is a smooth bottom finish. You cannot hope to go fast with weed and slime on the bottom, or, just as bad, a rough finish. Next time you are in a boatyard or marina look for one of the yachts whose name you have seen in the race results. Chances are her bottom finish will have been burnished glass-smooth.

On deck it will pay to mark the halyards for their correct tension and label the functions of all control lines. Once lines are marked it is simpler to repeat settings which have proven fast and having the crew know which lines do a particular job saves time and nervous energy. It is easier to obtain a better result by ensuring that set piece manoeuvres such as sail changes and gybes are faultless, rather than concentrating on the last fraction of an inch of sail trim.

It is the owner's responsibility to enter a race and, when entered, to decide whether to continue to race or not. The fact that a club may organize a race does not take away from the skippers the responsibility for their yachts. A skipper, therefore, should not only make sure the yacht is properly equipped but should ensure all the crew know the location of safety equipment and its operation.

For their part, the crew will expect the yacht to be properly equipped and organized. An allocation of tasks and a talk-through of each manoeuvre will help, even if the crew is a regular one.

OPPOSITE *When racing, intelligent positioning and a good start are essential.* BELOW LEFT *A port tack yacht must give way to a starboard tack yacht.*

RULES

Yachts racing together are governed by International Yacht Racing Union (IYRU) rules, though should their tracks cross, the International Regulations for Preventing Collisions at Sea (IRPCS) apply as normal.

The most important IYRU rules are contained in Sections B and C: Principle Right of Way Rules and Marks and Obstructions. In all, the IYRU racing rules cover 78 points ranging from simple definitions to protest procedures.

Those who race regularly will know most of the salient points. There are however, a few basic rules with which even the newcomer should be acquainted before he races. The rules exist, after all, to prevent collisions occurring and to encourage fair sailing. If racing yachts collide or if a right-of-way boat is forced to keep clear, the guilty yacht should either retire or accept the penalties as specified in the sailing instructions. If the guilty yacht does neither of these she may be protested by the innocent party, other competitors, or the race committee.

ABOVE *The windward yacht must keep clear of the yacht to leeward.*

ABOVE *Here the starboard tack yacht has right of way.*

THE FUNDAMENTAL RULES IN QUESTION ARE:

• In open water, a starboard-tack yacht has right of way over a port-tack yacht.
• A boat to windward keeps clear of a leeward boat.
• A boat tacking or gybing keeps clear of one which isn't.
• A boat clear astern keeps clear of one ahead when they are both on the same tack.
• When approaching a windward mark a port tack boat shall keep clear of a starboard-tack boat. If the boats are on the same tack, the boat on the inside shall be given room by the outside boat.
• When tacking around the mark, yachts must keep clear of any boats following.
• At the leeward mark a boat clear ahead of another has the right to gybe around the mark.
• At the start, the racing rules come into effect five minutes before the starting signal. At the starting mark, a boat overlapping to windward has no right to claim room when approaching the start line.
• Finally, a boat being overtaken by another has the right to protect her wind by luffing into it. This luffing right ceases when the helmsman of the windward yacht is level or forward of the mast of the leeward yacht.

THE START

It pays to reach the start area early to allow time for an assessment of wind and weather and select sails for the first leg. You will obtain course information from the committee boat at any time up until the five minute signal.

Various devices are used for the start sequence. In the USA shapes are most usual while flags are favoured in Britain. Whichever system is used a ten minute sequence is employed: the Warning Signal is displayed at ten minutes to go; the Preparatory Signal is displayed at five minutes to go; the Starting Signal is displayed at the end of the sequence. If more than one class is racing the Starting Signal of one class will be the Preparatory Signal of the next.

Strategically, a good start is vital. Get it right, and the rest of the fleet has to pass you. In ideal circumstances, the start will be from a committee boat with the line laid at precisely 90° to the wind direction. This should mean that neither side of the windward leg to the first mark is favoured. Often, however, the line is biased. A simple way to check is to luff head to wind next to the line and sight down it using the mainsheet traveller. Clearly, starting at the biased end of the line reduces the distance to the first mark. For the newcomer, however, a safe start is probably more important. This is almost certain to mean a starboard tack start and one away from the congested part of the line.

In club racing, the start line may be in line with two poles on the shore and the course may not even be upwind.

RACING UPWIND

When beating to windward in a fleet it is important to have clear air. If you have a yacht sitting forward and to weather of you, your yacht will receive 'dirty wind' and it nearly always pays to tack. The shortest route to the mark is the best one so you should look out for wind shifts. Within this overall shift the wind may oscillate from side to side. A shift which allows you to head closer to the mark is known as a lift and one which takes you away from the mark is called a header. Clearly it pays to tack on a header and to hold onto a lift.

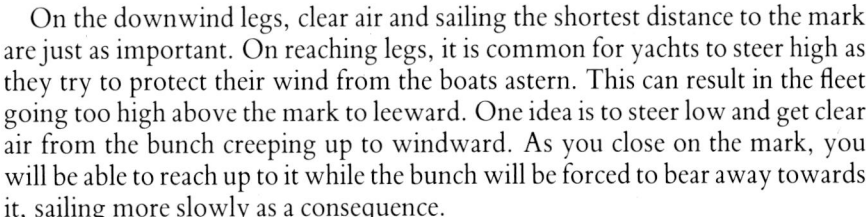

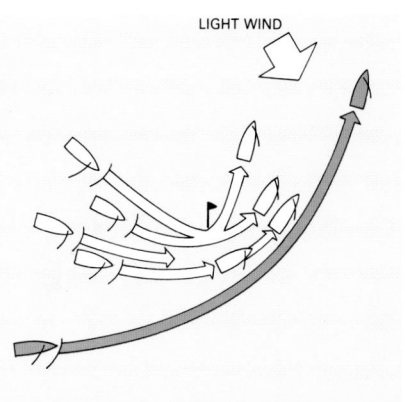

LIGHT WIND

LEFT *Rounding the mark, a crucial moment in any race.*
TOP *If space is tight at the mark, try skirting around the outside. The outer boat here handles a light air by staying clear of the pack, maintaining momentum and then reaching up for speed.*
ABOVE *The inside yacht has right of way if she has established a lead two lengths before the buoy.*

On the downwind legs, clear air and sailing the shortest distance to the mark are just as important. On reaching legs, it is common for yachts to steer high as they try to protect their wind from the boats astern. This can result in the fleet going too high above the mark to leeward. One idea is to steer low and get clear air from the bunch creeping up to windward. As you close on the mark, you will be able to reach up to it while the bunch will be forced to bear away towards it, sailing more slowly as a consequence.

When running, gybe onto the course nearest to the angle you need to steer towards the next mark. In light airs, it can pay to reach up a little as the extra distance sailed is often more than offset by the increase in speed. As before, spend more time on sailing the angle closest to the course required. Don't be afraid to gybe several times downwind to achieve this.

MARK ROUNDING

More places are gained and lost at marks than in any other parts of the race. The ideal mark rounding is similar to cornering a car. The corner, or buoy, is entered wide and the turn tightened to leave. You will also have picked the line into the buoy in good time, allowing for any tide pushing the yacht towards or away from the mark. If possible, give the crew plenty of time to prepare a spinnaker or different headsail for the next leg.

More often than not you will be in close company at the mark. Clearly the inside berth is best but if this is not possible, find an alternative which avoids you having to take an outside berth.

A win is the result of the following factors: preparation; a good start; clear air; sailing the best course dictated by wind and tide; clean mark rounding; and 100 per cent effort.

CHAPTER NINE

EMERGENCIES AFLOAT

The sea does not always offer sublime sailing; it can also deteriorate into a hostile environment. Although some emergencies cannot be foreseen, the prudent yachtsman plans to avoid the worst weather.

SEASICKNESS

Many sailors, experienced and inexperienced alike, are affected by seasickness. Even the great British Admiral, Lord Nelson, was a chronic sufferer and the only advantage experienced sailors have is the knowledge of how to mitigate its effects.

There are many drugs available on the market, although drowsiness is a common side effect. Recently, drugs which anaesthetize the inner ear have been made available as our balance mechanism in the ears' semi-circular canals has much to do with controlling motion sickness. Two examples of these drugs are Stugeron, available in the UK, and Transderm-Scop, increasingly available worldwide.

Simpler and more obvious ways to avoid sickness include not consuming excessive amounts of alcohol or rich foods. Proper clothing is also important as coldness exacerbates the condition.

Those suffering will often be lethargic, weak and may resist offers of help. If they are ill, they will probably be better kept warm below rather than crouching on deck to leeward. However, some individuals might prefer keeping a firm sight of the horizon. If so, put them in a safety harness and interest them in the running of the boat. A stint at the helm can be recuperative.

ABOVE *The crew should always be wary of overexposure to the sun.*
OPPOSITE *Top of the range oilskins for offshore sailing, with reflective patches and built-in harness.*

HYPOTHERMIA

Cold can kill. It is not necessary to fall overboard in order to feel the debilitating effects of cold. Many sailors will have experienced chilly watches and the expression 'feeling the cold in my bones' is very apt. Hypothermia is a decrease in the body's core temperature from its regular 98.4° fahrenheit (37°C).

Prevention is better than cure and a regular supply of hot drinks is beneficial. The ability to operate in the galley efficiently is therefore more important in foul conditions than in fair.

The symptoms of hypothermia are shivering, numbness, cramp and, as the condition deteriorates to critical levels, listlessness, slurred speech and abnormal behaviour. In the very worst cases the pupils dilate, the pulse becomes weak and breathing becomes difficult. Medical attention is imperative.

If these symptoms are detected among your crew, the patient should be gently rewarmed. Tepid drinks should be given but alcohol must be avoided at all costs. It may give a glowing sensation, but by stimulating the heart it merely transmits heat from the core to the surface where it is lost. The patient can be wrapped in a sleeping bag, although another source of heat inside the bag is helpful. The patient must of course be kept dry; evaporation of water on the skin's surface drains away heat.

FIRST AID

Besides having a well-stocked first aid kit on board you should also carry a manual, such as that published by the Red Cross organization. If you intend sailing regularly over long distances, then attending training courses is a sensible preparation.

At the very least you should be able to cope with common sailing accidents resulting in cuts, fractures and scalds. If you sail in waters where poisoning from marine life is common you should learn how to deal with this.

Above all, an understanding of emergency resuscitation is vital. Seconds count and there will be no time to thumb frantically through the manual.

If you are sailing with a new crew, find out whether they have any particular ailments. A diabetic, for instance, may need treatment which cannot be delayed until you return ashore.

The sun can be as much of a problem to the unwary as the cold. Combine a full day's sailing with the reflective effect of the sea and the result is a great deal more exposure to the sun than is normally experienced ashore. The problem is worsened by the fact that some of the best sailing areas in the world are located beneath a clean atmosphere and thus in strong and intense ultra-violet light.

Ensure that there is a good supply of suntan lotion, including total block. Pay particular attention to those areas which catch the sun most: nose; back of neck; shoulders; thighs; and tops of feet. Waterproof lotion is recommended: the combined effect of sunburn and salt spray is particularly painful.

The eyes must not be forgotten either. Without protection they can become sore, red and watery. Prolonged exposure can actually damage them.

HEAVY WEATHER

Few yachtsmen want to be caught out in heavy weather, although tough conditions to one might be enjoyable to another, depending on the size of their yacht, their level of experience and whether they are sailing upwind or downwind. Beating into a Force 5 breeze blowing against a two-knot tide can be difficult enough. Remember that forecast wind strengths are averages, so it is possible to experience gusts up to Force 7, even if a 5 was expected.

Preparation is the key. This can involve changing down sail sooner rather than later. It will help to have the next sail required stowed at the top of the locker or ready to hand below. It will also help to pre-cook hot food and have a supply of hot water or drink in a vacuum flask.

In planning your course you will need to allow for more leeway and to give yourself more sea room, particularly around headlands. Obviously, making sure that all hatches are secured, that the crew are properly clothed and wearing safety gear and that all loose gear is stowed is fundamental.

Avoiding bad weather is better than meeting it, so if you are able to reach shelter, do so. This will entail finding a place for which you have relevant charts, tide and approach information and making sure that you are not bringing the yacht into greater danger than you would be by staying at sea.

Sailing in rough conditions is difficult. If you are beating upwind you will probably be sailing into the waves, although an increase in wind associated with the passage of a front can bring a sudden wind shift and consequently a confused sea. A passage upwind can be smoothed out by steering up the face of waves and bearing away on their crest, so that the yacht slides down the back. This should reduce somewhat the spray thrown from the bow as you punch into the wave and make for a softer landing on its other side.

Steering downwind, the problem can be the yacht travelling faster than the waves themselves. Modern lightweight racing yachts can surf down the face of waves at great speed with an expert crew pushing the boat hard under lots of sail. With less sail set however, the yacht can be picked up by one wave, stopped

in the back of the next and then find her stern swung round by the following wave.

There are various techniques for dealing with heavy weather. Most require room to drift to leeward and there are no hard and fast rules as to which suits a particular type of yacht. When beating or reaching you may heave-to to ride out rough weather. This entails backing the jib (perhaps by tacking and not releasing the jib sheet) and tying the helm to leeward. The mainsail is then trimmed so that the yacht lies steadily with the bows pointing slightly upwind.

If the waves are large there could be a danger of their breaking onto the sails and putting undue strain on the rig. To avoid this you can lie-a-hull. The sails are dropped, securely stowed, the helm lashed to leeward and the yacht left to ride out the foul weather.

The motion may be too violent to make lying-a-hull tenable for long, in which case you may wish to run off downwind, although this will require a guiding hand on the helm. To slow the boat down and to give the helm something to bite against, it is possible either to stream a warp or a drogue. However, for either to be really effective they need to be long enough to stream two waves behind the yacht. Good fairleads and cleats are essential and to stand any chance of recovering, the warp or drogue will need to be led to the most powerful winch.

Several warps can be joined to form a loop so that the load can be spread from either quarter although a bridle will achieve the same effect. Recent research on drogues has shown that a cat's-cradle of light line across the neck of the drogue will stop it tangling up as it is rotated in the breaking crest of a wave. Such drogues can even be of help in moderate conditions to control the stern when crossing a bar guarding a harbour entrance.

When running away from the wind, some sail can be carried if there is sufficient room. A storm jib for instance, sheeted in hard on the centreline may help by holding the stern to the wind and seas.

BLOWN OUT SAILS

In rough conditions, both wind and wave action can damage the sails. The slightest tear or area of damaged stitching can extend quickly, especially if the sail is allowed to flog. Particular attention must be paid to chafe, especially on seams and edges. Carrying too large or too light a sail for the conditions also can cause damage.

As soon as damage is noticed the sail should be lowered straight away. To save it from flogging it will help to bear away when a headsail is dropped, protecting it in the lee of the mainsail. Dropping the mainsail requires keeping the boat moving under the headsail alone, as it will be difficult to haul the mainsail down while it is pressed against the rig.

A choice will have to be made whether to set another sail in place of the damaged one, or effect a repair. In the case of the mainsail it may be possible to reef it below the area of damage. If not, it will have to be stitched and then covered with self-adhesive sailcloth. Alternatively the trysail can be set, or, if one is not carried, a small jib set in similar fashion.

RIGGING DAMAGE

It is possible for part of the standing rigging to be damaged without losing the mast. However, swift action is required to take as much pressure as possible off the damaged area. For example, if a windward shroud fails, go about onto the opposite tack; if the forestay fails, bear away immediately and if the backstay fails steer upwind and sheet in the mainsail.

It is often possible to take a spare halyard or the topping lift out to a strong point on the deck and tension it as a substitute.

If conditions permit and the crew is experienced, it may be possible to send a person aloft in a bosun's chair. The motion aloft can be quite violent, so this is not a task to be undertaken lightly. If going up on a halyard do not use a snapshackle to attach the chair, use a screw-type shackle or a secure knot instead. A second halyard should be attached as a safety line and a rope on the underside of the chair to prevent it from swinging about. It is safest to have one person winding the winch and another tailing, so that the person in the chair can be watched all the time.

DISMASTING

Sometimes the damage may be so great that the mast bends or breaks in one or more places.

If you are dismasted, assess the situation immediately. Be careful as you move about on deck in case you trip over any of the debris: the yacht will have a much quicker and very different motion now that the damping effect of the rig has gone. First of all make sure that the mast, in particular the spreaders, are not going to punch a hole in the yacht as it rides the waves. In extreme circumstances, you may have to use bolt croppers and a hacksaw straightaway to cut the mast free, to save the yacht from sinking.

Normally, it ought to be possible to tie the mast steady. If you are drifting towards danger, do not start the engine until all the loose rope and wire has been secured, otherwise they might jam either the propeller or the rudder, or both. In shallow water, it may be possible to anchor.

If possible remove the sails if there is any chance that they can be used in a jury rig. Then unscrew, unshackle and cut your way through the standing rigging salvaging as much as you can. With luck, the boom can be removed and the remainder of the mast lashed aboard. If you are close to port and the engine is serviceable, you may be able to motor to safety. Outside assistance will probably not be necessary unless any of the crew is injured. If out at sea and with only limited fuel, you may be forced to build a jury rig when conditions improve.

When making a jury rig it will be easier if the top part of the mast with its sheaves and shroud attachment points can be used. If the original mast was keel-stepped it is likely that a stump will remain to which the section of mast can be lashed. If, however, there is no such stump, a means will have to be found to raise the section of mast into an upright position. One method is to use the boom or spinnaker pole as a bi-pod to create greater leverage on a rope raising the section. Jury rigging needs to be attached before the section is raised and if it is rope and not wire it can be tensioned more easily.

It may be possible to set a deep-reefed mainsail or two small headsails. You will not be able to steer much closer to the wind than 60° so seek a destination downwind.

There have been some remarkable achievements under jury rig. Solo sailors dismasted in mid-Atlantic have reached their original destination, while the yacht *Ceramco New Zealand* logged 16 knots in this condition when she broke her mast during the first leg of the 1981/2 Whitbread Round the World Race.

STEERING FAILURE

The majority of steering failures are caused not by the loss of the rudder blade but by the breakdown of the mechanism controlling it. (Most organisers of coastal races require an emergency tiller to be carried.) On wheel-steered yachts for instance, the problem is usually caused simply by the breaking of a link in the wire-chain system or by one of the cables jumping off a sheave. It is a sensible precaution to practise fitting your emergency tiller and seeing how the boat handles. Some tillers supplied as standard by boat builders are far from satisfac-

PROTECTION AGAINST ULTRA-VIOLET LIGHT

The strength of sunlight is deceptive at sea, when a cooling breeze is blowing. Its debilitating effects are exacerbated by reflection off the water and a clean atmosphere which does not block ultra-violet light.

OPPOSITE ABOVE *Dismasted during an inshore race.*
OPPOSITE BELOW *A 35 ft (11 m) yacht running before a mid-Atlantic gale.*

tory because they either foul deck gear or are so short that lines have to be rigged to them and led to winches to relieve the load.

If the blade itself is lost, first of all check to see that no water is coming in via the rudder stock.

A broken tiller is surprisingly difficult to replace as there are few suitable pieces of timber aboard and there is often a special fitting joining tiller to the head of the rudder. It makes sense, therefore, to carry a spare for both.

If wind vane self-steering is fitted it may be possible to use its servo rudder once the sail area is suitably reduced.

Some form of emergency steering may sometimes have to be rigged. Control can often be achieved by playing with sail trim: sheeting in the mainsail to bring the boat into the wind; sheeting in the headsail to bring the bow away from the wind. The effect might be enhanced by setting a jib on the backstay instead of using the mainsail, or by towing a drogue or bucket. For a jury rudder you will need to use the spinnaker or jib pole over the transom. On the outboard end attach a floorboard, locker top or something similar (this may be pre-drilled for just such an eventuality). The inboard end will need control lines led to blocks on either gunwhale and then to a winch. The pole should then pivot about a fulcrum created by lashing the pole to the backstay fitting, or a leg of the aft pulpit, so as to form a crude but effective rudder.

HULL DAMAGE

If the hull has been punctured good access through floorboards and lockers is vital. There are various ways to fill the hole and if you are able to pump the water out faster than it is coming in, there is a chance of reaching safety. It may be possible to heel the boat far enough to bring the hull clear of the water. You may be able to place a sail over the hole and secure it around the hull. If the hull curvature is not too extreme, try screwing a piece of plywood over the hole with self-tapping screws or perhaps shoring it in position with other floorboards. Other means of blocking large holes are with sailbags and bunk cushions, while small cracks, such as those around the keel caused by running aground, can be treated with epoxy paste. Most chandlers sell a variety which will set underwater.

There is a growing trend among builders of small to medium sized yachts to make them 'unsinkable'. This entails filling spaces between hull skins with positive buoyancy foam. Tests have shown such yachts will be awash, but not sink.

RUNNING AGROUND

Going aground is an everyday hazard, but not always serious unless it is caused by inaccurate navigation or carelessness. The immediate reaction of the helmsman should be to spin the boat round and see if she will come off the way she went on. If this fails, drop the sails to prevent her from driving on further, if it is a lee shore. On a weather shore, hoisting more sail may do the trick.

If the tide is flooding you may be floated free very quickly. If it is falling, you may be in for a long wait until the next high tide. The worst possible situation is to go aground at high water during a spring tide: then you may have to wait until the cycle of tides runs through neaps and back into springs, some two weeks later. If the tide is falling, it is a good idea to heel the boat towards the shore. This should not only make her sit more upright but lean the cockpit away from the incoming sea. There might be time to use cushions and sailbags to pad nasty looking rocks as the yacht heels towards them.

Several techniques may be used to get the boat off. One is to take an anchor out in the dinghy and then lead the rode to a winch via a block; another is to reduce the draft by suspending heavy weights such as jerry cans on the boom. Sinking the bow may also reduce draft, depending on the shape of the yacht. If a yacht has twin keels, however, remember it will draw less water upright than when heeled.

OPPOSITE *Running aground is something which may happen eventually even to the best skippers. If conditions are safe, crew members may try climbing out to the end of the boom in an attempt to heel the yacht and thereby reduce draft.*

MAN OVERBOARD

Losing a person over the side is probably the situation sailors fear most. Most crews will have had some experience of recovering a hat or bucket dropped overboard and will have realised the difficulties even in fair conditions. Practising man overboard drill is, therefore, an important safety precaution and the skipper is well advised to get other members of the crew to learn how to handle the yacht under such circumstances, in case it is the skipper himself who is lost over the side.

A cry of 'Man overboard' will alert the whole crew. Anyone below deck should press the appropriate button on the sophisticated navigation aid such as Decca Navigator or Loran, which will pinpoint the position and allow the vessel to return to the same spot. Failing this, a careful note of compass heading and log reading or time should achieve the same result. Simultaneously, on deck, the life belt should be thrown and, if fitted, the dan-buoy as well. A crew member should be detailed to watch the person all the time as the head and shoulders of a person in the water can be quickly lost from sight from even a slow moving yacht sailing in fair conditions.

Return to the person in the water as quickly as possible. If a spinnaker is set or the jib is poled out, these must be cleared away immediately. With the boat under normal sail again, she can be tacked or gybed onto a reciprocal course. Some skippers prefer to gybe as this takes the yacht downwind so that the person can then be approached on a close reach. Tacking may be safer if conditions are difficult and is less likely to disorientate the inexperienced crew. Either way, the object is to approach the person from windward, ideally bringing the boat to a halt with the wind spilt from the sails, and with the person on the lower side – the yacht's leeward beam. This calls for precise control of speed and course.

There is no reason why the engine should not be used but make absolutely certain that there are no sheets or ropes over the side to foul the propeller. To do so could inhibit the yacht from sailing back to the lost crew member.

THE DAN BUOY

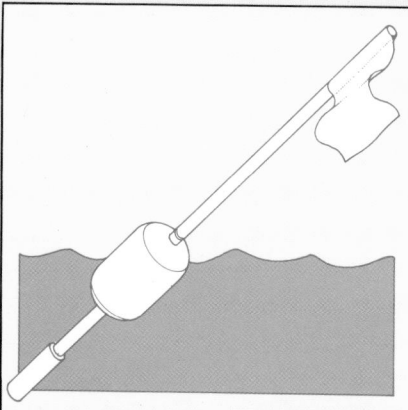

The Dan Buoy has a conspicuous flag about nine inches (25 cm) square, a plastic stave about six feet long, an 18-inch (50-cm) 'Thru-line' float and lead or steel ballast weighing between 10 and 15 pounds (4.5 to 7 kg).

Recovering the person from the water can be even more difficult. If the victim is still conscious and mobile, he might be able to climb up the stern ladder or use a rope looped over the side. If he is helpless, the difficulties are immense. It may be possible for another member of the crew to slip into the water (provided they are tethered to the yacht and wearing a lifejacket), to slip a safety harness or bowline around the victim. He can also be winched aboard using the main halyard. Such assistance should not be attempted if there is a chance of adding an additional problem to the first emergency.

In dealing with a man overboard, throwing the horseshoe lifebuoy to the crew member in distress is a first priority.

The most frequently used method for recovering a man overboard is to attach the luff of a sail to the gunwhale. A halyard is fixed to the clew and the sail lowered in the water like a scoop. Even a weak victim may be able to hold himself in the sail as it is raised on the halyard. As the sail is raised it

DISTRESS SIGNALS

There are several ways of signalling for help and these should be used only when the situation demands. Even with the high number of 'false alarms', most rescue services would prefer warning to be given early enough for them to respond in time.

VHF radio is perhaps the most commonly used means for indicating distress. Before you transmit you will need to know your position, which may be given as either latitude and longitude or, more simply, a distance and bearing from a known landmark or object. Transmit on Channel 16 at full power, following this procedure:

> • the distress signal MAYDAY MAYDAY MAYDAY
> • the name or other identification of the vessel in distress
> • particulars of her position
> • the nature of distress and the kind of assistance required
> • any other information which may facilitate the rescue
> • the invitation to reply and acknowledge

If no reply is received, check the equipment and repeat at regular intervals on the same channel or on any other channel.

If the safety of the yacht or person is not in immediate danger a less urgent message may be broadcast using the signal PAN PAN instead of MAYDAY.

If out of VHF range, or in mid-ocean, use either MF radio on the distress frequency of 2182 kHz or activate the EPIRB (Emergency Position Indicating Radio Beacon) which operates on aircraft frequencies.

If no radio is required visual signals can be used. These include: raising and lowering your arms slowly; thick black smoke generated by burning oily rags; an ensign hoisted upside down; a square flag with a ball, or similar, above or below it, or the morse code SOS (... _ _ _ ...).

The following International Code flags have specific meanings:

F	I am disabled
V	I require assistance
O	Man overboard

W	I require medical assistance
N C	I am in distress and require assistance

Lastly, virtually all yachts carry flares. They both draw attention to the boat and help locate it. White flares are for collision warnings, red flares are distress signals. There are three types of flares, namely: parachute rockets which reach 1000ft (300m) and which burn for 40 seconds; red hand flares which burn for 40 seconds; and buoyant orange smoke signals which burn for three minutes.

They should be used in the following order: two red parachute rockets fired two minutes apart, the first to attract attention and the second for verification. You should then wait at least 40 minutes for a response before firing more. If a vessel or helicopter is sighted, identify yourself with the red hand flare. The buoyant orange signal is also used for identification from the air.

At night a search aircraft may fire a green flare to which a red hand flare can be used as a response.

There are three musts in using flares. They *must* be in date. You *must* read the instructions. You *must* fire them downwind. Hand flares generate a lot of smoke and heat while parachute rockets are specially designed to assume an upwind trajectory. When there is low cloud cover, angle the rockets down to no more than 45°.

draws the person closer to the yacht and also increases in area to form a bigger envelope.

It may also be possible to use the boom and mainsheet as a gantry, but only if the topping lift is strong enough. Practise different methods in calm waters until you find one that works and become familiar with it.

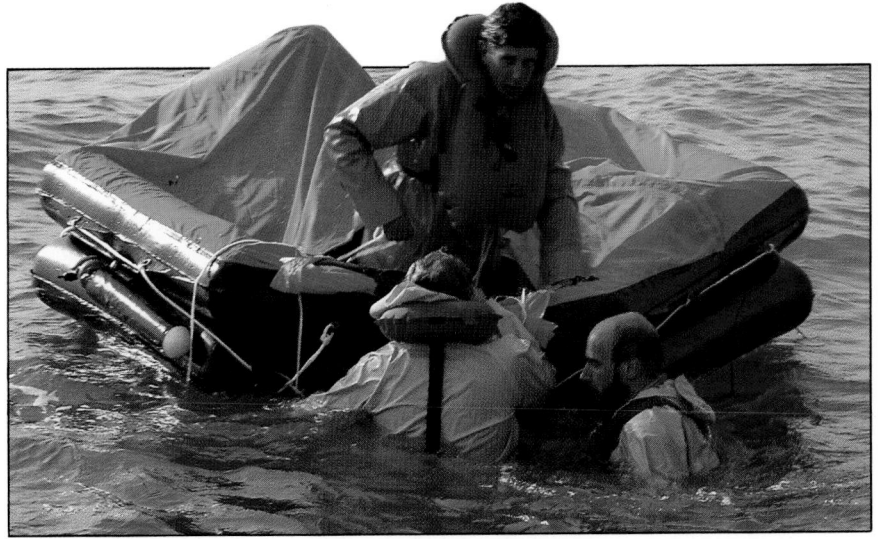

ABANDONING SHIP

If the yacht is in imminent danger of sinking, the liferaft must be launched but only as a last resort. In the 1979 Fastnet Race lives were lost from the liferafts of yachts which ultimately survived the storm.

When launching the raft, it is essential that the painter is made fast to the yacht so that the raft does not blow away as soon as it inflates. It is preferable to launch the liferaft to leeward so that there is a modicum of protection when it is boarded. An exception to this is a situation in which you are trying to escape from a fire; being upwind should then help you keep clear of the flames. Any gear to be taken aboard the raft should be tied to a crewmember wearing a lifejacket. Such gear could include flares in a waterproof container, an EPIRB and a 'panic bag' containing, for example, knife, chocolate, survival blanket, food rations and water.

If there is time, bail the raft out first so that the crew can board dry. It might be necessary however to clamber aboard from the sea or even right the liferaft itself first. To do this, stand on the gas bottle pocket and haul on the righting lines. At the doorway, there should be a ladder which sinks deep enough to enable you to grab the handle in the opening and pull your torso onto the top of the tube and roll in. Once in, it is probably better to shift your weight opposite the opening to steady the raft. Deploy the drogue as soon as you can because it contributes greatly to the stability of the raft.

CUTTING THE PAINTER

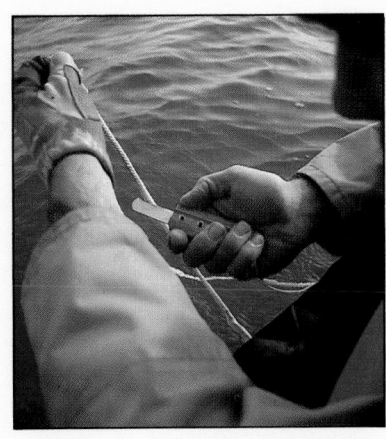

A knife is part of the liferaft kit, needed for cutting the painter. The painter is designed to break under a certain load, so that the raft will not be dragged under if the yacht sinks rapidly.

OPPOSITE ABOVE *Liferafts have water pockets to provide stability.*
OPPOSITE BELOW *Boarding the raft; before abandoning the yacht, don as much warm clothing as possible.*
ABOVE LEFT *If the raft is stable enough, first person in can help the others to board.*
BELOW LEFT *Inside the raft; it should be insulated and preferably have a double floor.*

NAVIGATION LIGHTS AND SHAPES

1 At anchor. *All-round white light.*

2 At anchor. *Black ball forward.*

3 Motor sailing. *Cone, point down, forward.*

4 Divers down. *Letter 'A' International Code.*

5 Vessel fishing. *All-round red light over all-round white.*

6 Fishing/trawling. *Two cones point to point, or a basket if less than 20 m.*

APPENDIX: RULES OF THE ROAD

Considering that man has been at sea since pre-history, it is surprising that the rules of the road were only formalised just over 100 years ago.

The International Regulations for the Prevention of Collision at Sea is the seaman's Highway Code. It is a complex, binding document which deals with every situation a vessel is likely to encounter, both on the high sea and arms of the sea.

The rules themselves are a masterpiece of drafting with each word having a precise meaning. 'May' gives the seaman an option while 'shall' and 'must' are mandatory. While the rules may appear daunting – there are 38 of them, each with many sub-sections – they do correspond to general common sense and seamanship.

Learning the rules word-perfect would be almost impossible, but every sailor is urged to study them in depth in order to appreciate fully their spirit and to learn the significance of lights, shapes and sound signals and the responses they require from those at sea.

Most national yachting authorities publish the full Collision Regulations with special annotation explaining points of special relevance. Britain's Royal Yachting Association (RYA) is one such example.

There are basically two types of rule:

1. Those which tell the yachtsman what to carry and how and when to use it. Some of these rules tell other mariners who you are, where you are, what you are doing and where you are going;

2. Those which tell the other mariner what his course of action should be, so that he can tell you what he is, where he is, what he is doing and where he is going.

This distinction between the two parties is fundamental to the Collision Regulations.

The rules are in four sections: General; Steering and Sailing Rules; Lights and Shapes; Sound and Light Signals.

What follows is an abridged version of the main rules. The rules themselves are in italics.

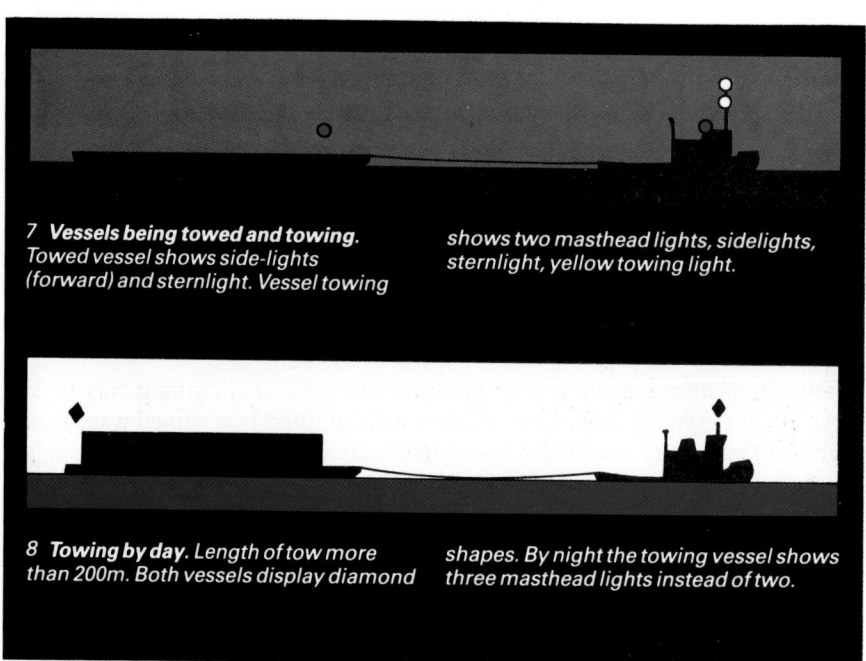

7 Vessels being towed and towing. *Towed vessel shows side-lights (forward) and sternlight. Vessel towing shows two masthead lights, sidelights, sternlight, yellow towing light.*

8 Towing by day. *Length of tow more than 200m. Both vessels display diamond shapes. By night the towing vessel shows three masthead lights instead of two.*

PART A – GENERAL
RULE 1 – APPLICATION

These rules shall apply to all vessels on the high seas and waters connected therewith, navigable by sea going vessels.

RULE 2 – RESPONSIBILITY

Nothing shall exonerate any vessel or the owner, master and crew from the consequences of neglect. In complying with these rules due regard shall be given to all dangers of navigation and collision and to any special circumstances which may make a departure from these rules necessary to avoid immediate danger.

PART B – STEERING AND SAILING RULES

SECTION 1 – APPLIED IN ANY CONDITION OF VISIBILITY
RULE 5 – LOOK-OUT

Every vessel shall maintain at all times, a proper look-out by sight and hearing as well as by all available means appropriate to the circumstances.

This is probably the single most important rule. On yachts you must be aware of the blind spots such as behind the leeward side of the headsail or behind the structure if keeping watch for long periods from an inside steering position. It is also important to preserve night vision from bright interior lights, cigarette lighters and deck floodlights because 100 per cent night vision is lost in a fraction of a second, yet takes many minutes to recover. Note also the reference to hearing. In fog, for example, a look-out away from engine and exhaust noise is invaluable.

RULE 6 – SAFE SPEED

Every vessel shall proceed at a safe speed so that she can take proper and effective action to avoid collision.

Many factors should be taken into account here: level of visibility, traffic density, manoeuvrability of vessels, depth of water, presence of background lights at night and state of wind, sea and tide.

RULE 7 – RISK OF COLLISION

In determining if the risk of collison exists, the following shall be among the considerations taken into account: if the compass bearing of an approaching vessel does not alter appreciably or if approaching is a very large vessel, a tow or vessel at close range.

Here there can be no substitute for taking a bearing on an approaching vessel and monitoring any change closely.

RULE 8 – ACTION TO AVOID COLLISION

Action to avoid collision shall be positive, made in ample time and with due regard to good seamanship.

This often means making your intentions clear early. In giving way to one vessel do not increase the risk of collision with another. In confined waters such alterations of course may often take small craft out of the buoyed deep water channels.

RULE 9 – NARROW CHANNELS

A vessel proceeding along the course of a narrow channel or fairway shall keep as near to the outer limit of the channel as is safe and practicable. A vessel less than 20 metres or engaged in fishing, shall not impede the passage of any other vessel and any vessel shall if

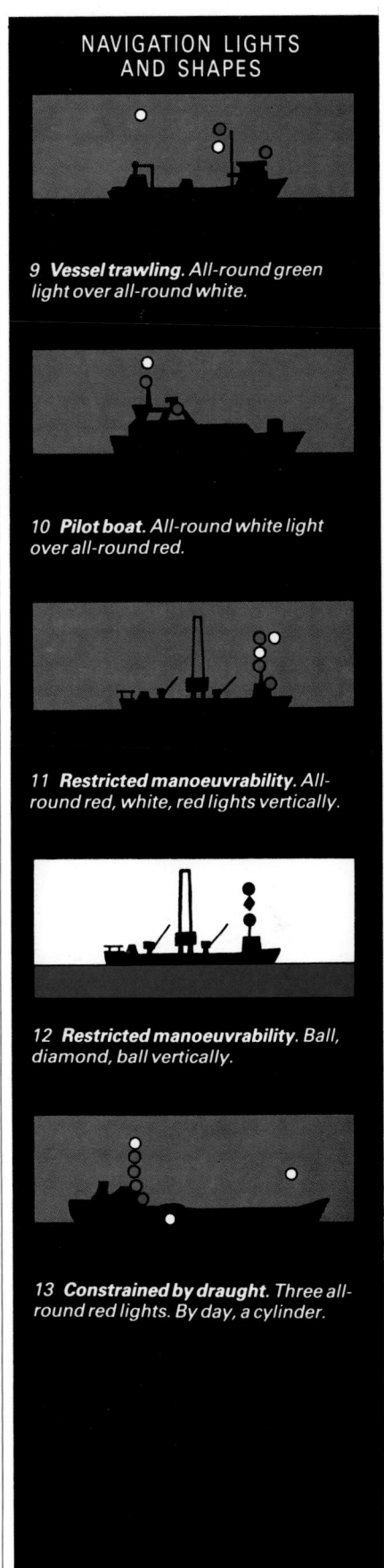

NAVIGATION LIGHTS AND SHAPES

9 Vessel trawling. All-round green light over all-round white.

10 Pilot boat. All-round white light over all-round red.

11 Restricted manoeuvrability. All-round red, white, red lights vertically.

12 Restricted manoeuvrability. Ball, diamond, ball vertically.

13 Constrained by draught. Three all-round red lights. By day, a cylinder.

possible avoid anchoring in the channel.

The definition of a narrow channel is purposely avoided. In what may seem a large body of water to the yachtsman, the professional mariner has to manoeuvre his merchant vessel with the utmost precision, while the area needed by a passenger liner to adjust speed or course is enormous.

RULE 10 – TRAFFIC SEPARATION SCHEMES

A vessel so far as practicable shall avoid crossing traffic lanes, but if obliged to do so, shall cross as nearly as practicable at right angles to the general direction of traffic flow. A vessel less than 20 metres or a sailing vessel shall not impede the safe passage of a power driven vessel following a traffic lane.

This last part may seem in conflict with the idea that power gives way to sail, but it should be obvious that a smaller vessel ought to keep clear of a larger one in an area of high traffic density. Also take special note of the instruction to cross at right angles. This means the yacht's heading (ie course steered) should be at right angles to the traffic lane, not her course over the ground.

There are two reasons for this. Firstly, simple geometry tells us that even if a yacht crabs sideways on a tide, she will cross through the lane quicker if she steers straight across rather than steering into the tide.

Secondly her aspect, particularly her lights at night, will show others that her intention is to cross at right angles. Traffic separation lanes are becoming increasingly frequent so our behaviour in them warrants extra thought.

SECTION 2 – CONDUCT OF VESSELS IN SIGHT OF ONE ANOTHER

RULE 12 – SAILING VESSELS

When two vessels are approaching one another, so as to involve the risk of collision, one of them shall keep out of the way of the other as follows:
i) When each has the wind on a different side, the vessel which has the wind on her port side shall keep clear.
ii) When both have the wind on the same side, the vessel which is to windward shall keep out of the way of the vessel to leeward.
iii) If a vessel with the wind on the port sees a vessel to windward and cannot determine with certainty whether the other has the wind on the starboard side, she shall keep out of the way of the other.

RULE 13 – OVERTAKING

Notwithstanding anything contained in the rules of this section, any overtaking vessel shall keep out of the way of the vessel being overtaken. A vessel shall be deemed to be overtaking when coming on another vessel from a direction more than 22.5 degrees abaft her beam. If a vessel should be in doubt as to whether she is overtaking or not, she should assume this is the case. Any subsequent alteration of the bearing between the two vessels shall not make the overtaking vessel a crossing vessel within the meaning of the rules.

This rule makes abundantly clear its priority over other Sailing and Steering rules. It also cautions the helmsman to assess the effect of a course alteration before it is made.

RULE 14 – HEAD-ON SITUATION

When two power driven vessels are meeting on a reciprocal course or nearly reciprocal courses, each shall alter her course to starboard so that each shall pass on the port side of the other.

For the purposes of the rules, a yacht using her auxiliary engine is considered a power driven vessel.

ABOVE *A thorough knowledge of the collision regulations will help you to decide without hesitation what to do when approaching commercial shipping.*

RULE 15 – CROSSING SITUATION

When two power driven vessels are crossing so as to involve the risk of collision, the vessel which has the other on her starboard side shall keep out of the way and shall, if the circumstances of the case permit, avoid crossing ahead of the other vessel.

One circumstance where this might apply is if a third ship or navigational hazard prevents an alteration to starboard.

RULE 16 – ACTION BY GIVE-WAY VESSEL

Every vessel which is directed to keep clear of another vessel shall, so far as possible, take early and substantial action to keep well clear.

RULE 17 – ACTION BY STAND-ON VESSEL

a) Where one of two vessels is to keep out of the way, the other shall keep her course and speed. The latter vessel however may take action to avoid collision by her manoeuvre alone, as soon as it becomes apparent to her that the vessel required to keep out of the way is not taking the appropriate action.

This rule may seem contradictory in that it requires the right-of-way vessel to maintain her course and speed but allows her to take avoiding action and ultimately requires her to avoid collision. The key is that it allows the stand-on vessel with rights, to take avoiding action if the give-way vessel fails to act in accordance with the rules. Thus a yacht should not hold on into danger just because the rules say she has right of way. Yachts even in daylight may be difficult to spot from a merchant ship and may not be sighted in time for the early action required of the give-way vessel by the rules to be taken.

RULE 18 – RESPONSIBILITIES BETWEEN VESSELS

Except where rules 9, 10 and 13 otherwise require:
a) a power driven vessel underway shall keep out of the way of a vessel not under command: a vessel restricted in her ability to move; a vessel engaged in fishing; a sailing vessel.
b) a sailing vessel shall keep clear of a vessel not under command; one restricted in her ability to manoeuvre; or one engaged in fishing.
c) a fishing vessel shall keep clear of vessels not under command and vessels with restricted ability to manoeuvre.

This is really a very logical rule requiring more manoeuvrable vessels to give way to those less so.

S O U N D   S I G N A L S

	POWER DRIVEN VESSELS IN SIGHT OF EACH OTHER
●	I am altering course to starboard
● ●	I am altering course to port
● ● ●	I am going astern
● ● ● ● ●	I fail to understand your intention or action; or I do not think that
	you are taking sufficient action to avoid collision
⬤	Warning by vessel approaching a bend
	VESSELS IN REDUCED VISIBILITY
⬤	Power driven vessel making way
⬤ ⬤	Power driven vessel stopped or not making way
⬤ ● ●	Sailing vessel or powered vessel restricted in its ability to manoeuvre,
	constrained by draught, under tow, or engaged in fishing

KEY   ● *denotes approximately 1 second*   ⬤ *denotes 4–6 seconds*

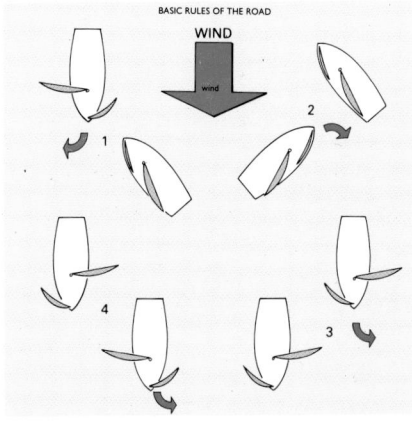

Basic rules of the road. 1 A boat running downwind gives way to one running close-hauled. 2 A boat on port tack gives way to one on starboard tack. 3 An overtaking boat must give way to the overtaken boat. 4 If two boats are running downwind, the one on starboard tack has right of way.

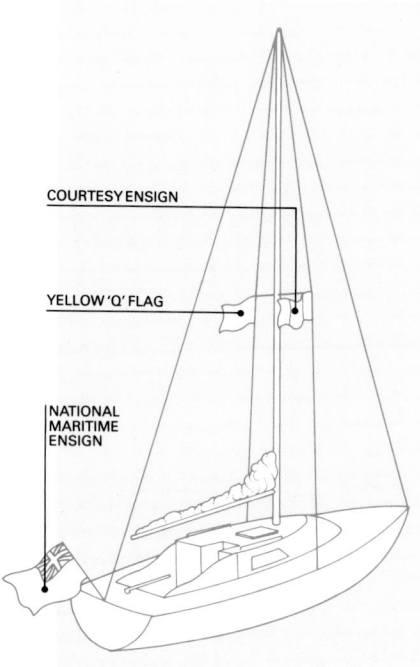

COURTESY ENSIGN

YELLOW 'Q' FLAG

NATIONAL
MARITIME
ENSIGN

ABOVE *Flag positions.*

CUSTOMS AND ETIQUETTE

Yachting has a fine tradition behind it, though naturally many things change over the years. It also has a name for being a courteous sport and the rules under which we race are based on sportsmanship. There cannot be many sports in which, at the most competitive level, fair play is left to the competitors themselves rather than it being put in the hands of a 'referee'. At the end of a race for instance, it is common practice to sign a declaration that the rules of the game have been adhered to.

Courtesy on the water is something which sailors value highly. As the pace of life becomes more frenetic ashore, the goodwill experienced in the company of other sailors is valued more highly than ever.

ENSIGNS

More custom surrounds flags than probably any other facet of yachting, and few subjects occupy yarning sailors more than precisely the 'right' way to do things.

One fact, however, is certain: of all flags flown it is the ensign which denotes the nationality of the yacht and her owner and use of the national maritime flag is governed by law around the world. Today though, establishing the actual nationality of the owner is not so straightforward, for many yachts are company owned. It is common for large luxury motor yachts to wear the British Red Ensign, for example, because of the status it brings, though the company owning the yacht may be foreign-owned.

For small pleasure craft, wearing their country's maritime ensign is usually optional unless they are registered. At sea, the ensign (or colours) is worn during daylight hours. In port, the hours are considered to be 0800 until 2100 or sunset, whichever is soonest. It is the traditional practice to take one's time for making colours and for striking them from naval vessels which might be in port or from the senior yacht club. Sadly, many of today's owners leave their ensign flying all day, all night and even when they pack up and leave the yacht.

Some yachts have the right to wear special status ensigns. In Britain, for example, a special Admiralty warrant can be obtained to wear the White Ensign or the Blue or Red Ensign which have been 'defaced' with a club crest. Such privilege ensigns can only be flown when the owner is onboard.

Ensigns are the most important flags a yacht can wear, so they should be flown in the most prominent position. Surprisingly this is the aft end, not the bow, dating from the time when sailing ships were commanded from the quarter deck. On a sloop, a staff on the taff rail can be used. Yawls and ketches use a staff on top of the mizzen mast, while gaff-rigged yachts and schooners should attach the ensign two-thirds up the leech of the aftermost sail.

FLAG OFFICERS AND CLUB BURGEES

The notion of seniority governs the use of other flags. Yachts often fly their club burgees (small triangular flags) at the masthead and if an owner belongs to more than one, he should fly the burgee of the more senior club, or the club whose home port he is visiting. Most yacht clubs have special flags for their officers, based on the club burgee. The commodore can fly a broad or swallow-tailed pennant (long tapered flag) while those belonging to the vice- and rear-commodores are distinguished by one or two balls being added to the design.

COURTESY AND Q FLAGS

When visiting foreign waters it is courteous to fly the maritime ensign of that country. It should be smaller than the yacht's own national flag and flown in an inferior position. Most often, this will mean from the starboard spreader. When entering foreign waters for the first time, or when returning to home waters from abroad, the yellow Flag 'Q' should be flown from the port spreaders. This indicates a request for Customs clearance.

SALUTING

It is a custom to salute royal yachts and warships of all countries and yachts belonging to flag officers of the owner's own club. Fortunately the latter has only to be done once in a day. To make a salute, the ensign is 'dipped'. This entails lowering the ensign to a little lower than half hoist and keeping it there until the vessel being saluted responds in similar fashion. When the latter re-hoists her ensign, the saluting vessel follows suit.

DRESSING SHIP

If a full set of International Code flags are carried a yacht may 'dress ship'. This is decorative and in Britain is done on the Queen's birthday. Other occasions are festivals at home and abroad and local events, such as club regattas or cruising meets. There are few finer sights than a yacht dressed from stem to masthead to stern. The preferred order from bow to stern uses signal flags and numeral pennants. The suggested order is:

E Q p3 G p8 z p4 W p6 P p1 I Code T Y B X 1st H 3rd D F 2nd U A O M R p2 J p0 N p9 K p7 V p5 L C S.

ABOVE *Dressing ship for the club regatta.*

ETIQUETTE AT SEA

The unwritten laws of etiquette aim to prevent one yachtsman spoiling the enjoyment of another. For instance, careless disposal of rubbish at sea spoils the water for everyone, including the wildlife. When passing yachts racing it is courteous to take avoiding action and pass to leeward of them even if you have right of way under the collision regulations. You should in any case be rewarded by a friendly wave and hail of thanks: unfortunately, too many racing sailors expect such avoidance almost as a right.

Whenever you see another yacht in difficulty, see if you can offer assistance. If she is in distress you are bound to by law, but there are other times where the offer of a tow, some spare fuel or fresh water would be gratefully accepted.

ETIQUETTE IN HARBOUR

Yachtsmen have more opportunities to help each other in port. When you see a boat come in for example, you can offer to take her lines as she berths.

If you intend going alongside another yacht you should ask permission first and find out if her departure plans are compatible. It might be worth considering mooring the opposite way round to your neighbour. This will help the yachts lie alongside each other more easily, separate the masts in case they swing together and give a little more privacy to those sitting in either cockpit. If you need to cross other boats to go ashore, always pass forward of the mast so as not to disturb those in the cockpit or those below. Similarly, on returning from the shore be careful not to walk any debris aboard.

At night noise carries great distances across the water so don't let your enjoyment spoil that of others. If you wish to speak to someone on board another yacht it is courteous to knock on the deck or topsides rather than appear at the companionway without warning.

When visiting an area, it is always considerate to look in at the local yacht club and introduce yourself. Most clubs welcome guests and let them use their facilities.

GLOSSARY

A

ABAFT behind
ABEAM at right angles to the centreline
A-HULL to lie with no sails set
ANGEL weight suspended on anchor cable
APPARENT WIND true wind speed and direction modified by boat's movement
ASTERN behind the boat or moving backwards
ATHWARTSHIPS at right angles to the fore-and-aft line

B

BACKSTAY stay supporting the mast from aft
BALLAST weight used to add stability
BARE POLES underway with no sails set
BATTEN wood or plastic stiffening in leech
BEAM maximum width or an object at right angles to the middle of the boat
BEAR AWAY to turn away from the wind
BEARING the direction of an object from the observer
BEAT to sail close-hauled
BERTH place where boat is moored or place to sleep on board
BILGE that part inside the hull above and around the keel where water will collect; also curved part of hull below the waterline
BI-LIGHT navigation light showing two functions
BITTER-END the end of the rope which is not made fast
BLOCK a pulley around which rope or wire runs
BOLLARD a short post around which ropes are secured
BOOM wooden or metal spar controlling mainsail foot
BOTTLESCREW threaded rigging screw
BOW forward part of the boat
BOW ROLLER fitting over which anchor chain runs
BOWER anchor used at the bow
BROAD REACH see reach
BUNT fold of sail resulting from reefing
BUOY floating object for mooring or navigation
BURGEE small masthead flag

C

CABLE chain or rope attached to anchor
CATAMARAN twin-hulled vessel
CENTREBOARD metal or wooden board lowered through keel to stop leeway
CENTRELINE fore-and-aft line running through middle axis of boat
CLEAR AIR wind unaffected by other yachts or objects
CLEAT fitting around which rope is secured
CLEW bottom after corner of sail
CLOSE-HAULED sailing as close as possible to the wind as in beating
CLOSE REACH see reach
COAMING raised superstructure around cockpit
COCKPIT well in deck where helmsman and crew work
COMPANIONWAY access from deck to cabin
CRINGLE eyelet in corner of sail

D

DISPLACEMENT the weight of water equal to the weight of the boat or description of the boat's weight
DOWNHAUL control rope to pull down a spar or sail
DOWNWIND to leeward or to sail before the wind
DRAFT (DRAUGHT) depth of boat from bottom of keel to water line or amount of camber (curve) in a sail
DROGUE sea anchor made from rope and cloth to retard drift

E

ENSIGN flag showing nationality
EYE OF THE WIND true direction of wind

F

FAIRLEAD fitting which guides direction of rope or line
FENDER soft plastic buoy to protect side of vessel
FETCH to reach towards the wind
FLAKE to lay out rope or chain in tight zig-zag pattern
FLOOD a tide coming in, opposite of ebb
FLUKE part of anchor designed to pierce sea bed
FOOT bottom edge of sail
FORE forward
FORESTAY stay supporting the mast from forward
FREEBOARD height of yacht from waterline to deck edge

G

GAFF spar supporting top of mainsail
GALLEY compact kitchen aboard a vessel
GENOA large headsail which overlaps the front of the mainsail
GOOSENECK universal joint between boom and mast
GOOSEWING sailing downwind with mainsail to leeward and headsail to windward
GROUND TACKLE anchor and chain
GUY steadying rope for a spar
GYBE to tack with the stern of the yacht passing through the wind

H

HALYARD rope used to hoist and lower a sail
HANK fitting used to attach sail luff to a stay
HAWSE PIPE pipe for feeding anchor chain through foredeck to locker below
HEADSAIL sail forward of the mast attached to the forestay
HEAVE-TO position used in heavy weather with the jib backed to leeward
HEEL leaning of a vessel to one side due to wind or sea
HELM means of steering a yacht, eg wheel or tiller

I

INSHORE sheltered waters close to coast

J

JACKSTAY wire span attached to deck to which safety harnesses can be attached
JIB headsail set forward of mast
JURY improvised gear to replace damaged mast or rudder for example

K

KEDGE a back-up anchor smaller than the main one
KEEL fin or fins used to carry ballast and offer lateral resistance against leeway
KETCH twin-masted vessel with mizzen mast ahead of rudder post
KICKING STRAP tackle used to control upward pull of boom

L

LANYARD a short light line for making objects secure
LEECH after edge of a sail
LEE HELM tendency of a boat to bear away from the wind
LEE SHORE a shore onto which the wind is blowing
LEEWARD away from the wind
LEEWAY sideways slipping of a boat due to wind pressure from opposite side
LOA length overall
LOG distance measuring device or navigator's document of record
LORAN long range navigation system based on the measurement of the difference in time of reception of signals from a pair of shore transmitters
LUFF front edge of sail; or to steer into the wind
LUFF FOIL metal spar around forestay into which sails are fed
LUFF GROOVE slot to hold sail in either luff foil or mast

M

MAINSAIL the principal sail set on the mast
MARK course marker during a race
MASTHEAD RIG rig in which jibs are set from the top of the mast
MIZZEN the after mast or sail in ketch or yawl rig
MONOHULL vessel with one hull
MOOR to tie up a vessel to a fixed point or to lie to two anchors
MULTIHULL vessel with more than one hull eg catamaran or trimaran

N

NAVEL PIPE see hawse pipe
NEAP TIDE the least tide in a lunar month

O

OFF THE WIND to sail downwind
ON THE WIND beating or close-hauled
OFFSHORE some distance off the land
ONE-DESIGN a class of yachts to identical design
OUTHAUL rope used to tension the foot of a sail
OVERHANGS the ends of a boat above the waterline

P

PAINTER a line for securing the bow of a dinghy
POINT OF SAILING course of the boat relative to the wind direction eg beating

PILOT a guide containing navigation and harbour approach information etc
POINTING a boat's heading relative to the wind when beating
PONTOON floating jetty
PORT left hand side of a vessel when looking forward
PULPIT metal guardrail at bow

Q

QUARTER portion of vessel between beam and stern
Q FLAG yellow rectangular International Code Flag requesting Customs clearance

R

RAKE the amount by which a mast leans backwards or forwards from the vertical
RDF radio direction finding
RIG general term to describe sails, spars and rigging
REACH to sail at more or less right angles to the wind eg broad reach, sailing with the wind abaft the beam and with sails well out on the quarter (the after part of the yacht's side); or close reach, sailing nearly close-hauled with sheets just eased
REEF to reduce the area of the sail
REEF PENDANT line used to pull down a reef
RUNNING to sail directly away from the wind
RUNNING RIGGING the ropes or wires used to set and adjust sails eg halyards and sheets

S

SAMSON POST stout post on foredeck to which mooring lines are attached
SCHOONER sailboat with two or more masts in which the mainmast is behind the smaller one or ones
SCOPE length of rope or chain paid out when anchoring
SEACOCK through hull valve for taking in water and discharging waste
SELF-TAILER type of winch which grips the rope automatically
SHACKLE metal joining link with screw-in closure
SHANK long central arm of an anchor
SHEAVE grooved wheel in a block, around which rope or wire turns
SHEET rope for trimming a sail eg mainsheet
SHROUD fixed rigging to support the mast athwartships
SKEG part of hull supporting leading edge of rudder

SLOOP single-masted rig with mainsail and headsail
SNUB to pull in a rope so as to bring it briefly under tension
SPINNAKER triangular sail set in front of the forestay when sailing downwind
SPREADER strut at side of mast to accept compression exerted by shrouds
SPRING a warp used to resist fore and aft movement of moored yacht
STANCHION metal post at deck edge to support guardrails
STARBOARD right hand side of a vessel when looking forward
STAYS wire or rope used to support mast
STEM the hull at the bow

T

TACK bottom front corner of sail or to turn the yacht from one side of the wind to the other
TAFFRAIL guard rail at stern
TENDER small dinghy or description of yacht which heels easily
TOPPING LIFT line from masthead used to support the boom
TRANSIT the lining up of two objects
TRANSOM the after part of the hull between the waterline and deck level
TRI-LIGHT navigation light
TRAVELLER track for adjusting position of mainsheet athwartships
TRIM to adjust a sail or the flotation of the yacht; the way a yacht sits in the water
TRIPPING LINE a line to release an anchor or a fitting remotely
TURNBUCKLE threaded screw used to maintain correct tension on standing rigging; same as bottlescrew
TRYSAIL small storm sail set abaft the mast

U

UPHAUL a line for hauling up a spar

V

VANG see kicking strap

W

WARPS long ropes for mooring a boat
WEATHER HELM tendency of a boat to steer into the wind
WINCH mechanical device for hauling in sheets or halyards
WINDLASS mechanical device for hauling in anchor chain
WINDWARD upwind of the vessel

INDEX